REACHING FOR G-D

THE JEWISH BOOK ON SELF HELP

RABBI LAZER GURKOW

Boruch Hashem   *

REACHING FOR G-D
THE JEWISH BOOK ON SELF HELP

Copyright © 2012 Rabbi Lazer Gurkow
All rights reserved.

For interviews with the author, or to purchase this book in volume,
email: rabbi@innerstream.org

ISBN-13: 978-0615657837
ISBN-10: 0615657834

TABLE OF CONTENTS

ACKNOWLEDGEMENTS

Writing, completing and publishing a book is a mammoth task only undertaken with the support of a dedicated and professional team. No book is written in a vacuum and neither was this one; it would not have been completed without the assistance, guidance and encouragement of many special people. My debts of gratitude are many; the following is but a partial list of those whose contributions have greatly enhanced the quality of this work :

First and foremost, to my mother in law, Mrs. Leah Block, who generously reviewed the manuscript and whose input was invaluable. Your kind advice and gentle corrections streamlined the text and enhanced its clarity. May your kindness be repaid manifold by Hashem.

To my copy editor and proof reader Mrs. Yocheved Krems from Diamond Editing and to her colleague, who prefers to remain anonymous. Your wise council and professional guidance have polished the diamonds and improved the pages of this book. You have invested many hours and ably nudged author and manuscript to new and improved condition.

To my friends, who have graciously sponsored much of this project and who prefer to remain anonymous.

To my wife, Basie, who continues to be my partner in everything I do. You are an inexhaustible source of encouragement and support. Without your constant motivation this book would not have been written. Your kindness has humbled and encouraged me and can be repaid only by Hashem.

To my teacher and mentor the Lubavitcher Rebbe OBM; my source of inspiration and teaching. His unceasing leadership and devotion have motivated me to share what little I know. His love and dedication have inspired me; I pray that I be worthy of the title, Chassid.

Last, but not least, to Hashem, for giving me the wisdom, courage and stamina to bring this book to fruition. It is an incredible privilege to be a conduit of Torah learning; I am grateful for the opportunity and awed by the merit.

Finally, to my readers to whom this book is dedicated. May this book become a true learning experience. May it enhance your dedication to Torah and your relationship with Hashem. If even one reader is inspired to one more Mitzvah or another hour of Torah study, my reward will be complete.

FOREWORD

Self help books line many shelves in libraries and book stores. These books cover the entire spectrum of subjects and empower us to succeed. They train us to raise children, find happiness, nurture health; there is hardly a subject not covered by this genre.

Sadly, Judaism is the one subject on which there is little self help literature in the English language. There is good reason for this. Judaism was delivered with its own self help manual; the Torah. Guidance on every subject related to life, faith and observance is found in the Torah.

The Torah is accessible to all, but mining its pearls and finding creative ways to make them relevant in a modern age requires scholarship and training. Absorbing the surface, literal meaning of the Torah is not difficult, but plumbing its depths is another matter altogether. The Torah's wisdom is often hidden beneath layers of understanding; each layer revealing a depth, not previously discernible.

Generations of Torah scholars have enhanced our understanding of Torah immeasurably. Their writings enable us to peel back the Torah's layers and find the inner stream of meaning that flows beneath the text. As a rabbi, my primary goal is to bring these hidden layers of meaning to the surface so that they inspire and enlighten.

People often lament that they would love to take their observance to a new level, but aren't sure they have it in them to change. Another popular concern is that our observance lacks vibrancy; it's lackluster and almost by rote. The Torah teaches that we each have a wellspring of untapped potential within our soul that can empower and energize. We can not only believe in G-d, but also love Him. We can not only serve G-d, but also know Him. We don't have to look for this ability elsewhere; it is already within. All we need to do is unlock it.

This book is designed to give you the key. Drawing on the teachings of our forbearers, the essays in this book will show you how to tap into the boundless sacred energy that resides within you. It will help you unleash your Divine spark and show you how to bring the dynamism of your soul into the observance and ritual of every day.

This book will show you the way, but you need to walk the path. No one can walk it for you. First you need to decide that you are capable of success and next you need to decide that you are willing to make the effort. If you devote yourself to this effort you will surely succeed. "For this matter is not distant from you; [it is] in your mouth and in your heart to accomplish it." (Deuteronomy 30:14.)

INTRODUCTION

The essays in this book are organized according to subject. Each essay has a two line introduction that reviews the conclusions of the previous essay and lays out the question or point that follows from that conclusion. This point becomes the catalyst for the following essay, which develops the subject further.

Each essay is followed by a short summary that will challenge you to apply the essay to your own life and enhance your connection with your own center – your reservoir of G-dliness within.

The book is divided into four sections. Each section addresses multiple subjects.

Part one: Struggles and Temptation.

> This section begins with discipline. It is a series of essays that speaks to our obligation and more important our ability to overcome temptation and focus our lives toward holiness.

> The second series of essays argues that holiness is not beyond our reach – one need not seek it in the heavens; G-d is available right here on earth.

> Next the book turns to repentance and growth. No matter how holy or mundane our past, we are each on a growth trajectory. Growth is essential to life. And though the task seems daunting it is eminently doable.

Part Two: The Soul's Bond with G-d

> We now move to the subject of our inherent bond with G-d. Sometimes our lifestyle does not at all reflect our intrinsic bond with G-d; still, that bond is immutable. This series of essays provides concrete suggestions on how to enhance our awareness of this inherent, but often inexplicable bond.

The next subject in this section deals with the interplay of surrender and self reliance. Our bond with G-d suggests that G-d takes care of everything and we need not worry, yet we know we are expected to do for ourselves. How does one reconcile the two imperatives?

The next series of essays speaks to the issue of surrender. Surrendering to G-d is easy to speak of, but difficult to achieve; especially in times of suffering. These essays offer a number of suggestions to help us overcome the obstacles.

Part Three: Humility, Unity and Love

Humility

The book now turns to humility. I can pay lip service to my powerful soul, but deep in my heart I know my failings. I know that I cannot be like Moses. Is this a barrier between me and G-d?

Also, Judaism seems almost entirely about G-d. Is there any room for me? Are such questions allowed in Judaism?

Unity

This section deals with the distinct value of the individual and the collective value of the Jewish nation. A series of questions are then addressed. How is unity fostered? How can we respond with love to those who treat us with hatred? What is our common denominator?

Love

The book now offers a series of essays on love. What does it mean to truly love G-d? How is love for G-d different from love of a spouse? If G-d wanted us to love Him, why did He not make life easier for us?

Part Four: Miscellaneous Questions

As its heading implies this section deals with a number of questions that trouble us as humans and as Jews.

I have made an effort to present these nuanced and complex subjects in easily understood language. It is my hope that this book will serve to inform and inspire. The exhaustive sources available in the footnotes are intended to give you further food for thought and avenues for study.

Please note that when referring to the Almighty in this book I have used the name G-d. As is customary in many Jewish communities I have refrained from spelling out the name in full as a mark of reverence and respect for the Almighty.

This collection of essays is culled from my website, www.innerstream.org. When you have completed this book I invite you to peruse my website where you will find many more essays on the delightful layers of depth found in Jewish subjects and the, often unexpected, ways in which they are applied to our times.

I conclude with wishing us all success in this endeavor. It is the most important goal in life and the very purpose of our creation.

Rabbi Lazer Gurkow
London Ontario
Canada

PART ONE – OF STRUGGLE AND TEMPTATION

"Why did G-d give me temptation? What purpose can it possibly serve?"

INTRODUCING TEMPTATION

Babies are born innocent. So long as they're not exposed to candy, for instance, they don't crave it. But the moment they experience their first taste of candy, their innocence evaporates and a lifelong struggle to overcome temptation is underway. No longer can they eye such foods without experiencing an instant urge to indulge. Wise parents shelter their children from such temptation and prolong their child's innocence as long as they can.

It's interesting that G-d did not do the same for Adam and Eve.

DON'T EAT THE FRUIT, BUT ENJOY THE BARK

In their original state, Adam and Eve were innocent. Crafted by G-d's hand, they entered this world untainted, and would never have considered straying from G-d's Will. Yet, rather than shelter them, G-d left the door open for them to sample a variety of tempting tastes, including the one that would lead to their downfall. Placed in the Garden of Eden, Adam and Eve were surrounded by beautiful trees that produced delicious fruit and aromatic fragrance. They were permitted, and even instructed, to partake of the fruit of every tree in the garden, except for the one at the center of the garden.[1] Placing them in such a situation was akin to a parent setting a candy dish in front of his child, encouraging him to sample every candy, except for the most attractive one.

In fact, our Sages inform us that the specific conditions in the Garden of Eden posed an even greater challenge. The bark of the Tree of Knowledge was edible and tasted exactly like its fruit. Adam and Eve were permitted to drink

---

[1] *Genesis* 2:8–17.

the sap from this bark, and in doing so would naturally discover the delicious taste of the tree's fruit. At the same time, the fruit itself was forbidden.[2] This made the test that much more difficult. It's like a child who is placed before the same candy dish, but this time is permitted to lick the sweet wrapper of the forbidden candy, yet must leave the candy itself untouched. Why did G-d expose Adam and Eve to such temptation?[3]

THE INNER STRUGGLE

The answer lies in the virtue of achievement through struggle. G-d does not want ideal servants, naturally flawless in their devotion. (After all, he already has countless hosts of angels, who are just that.) He wants humans, creatures prone to temptation, who struggle mightily to overcome those temptations. He desires us with our weaknesses as well as our strengths. In the absence of struggle, the extent of our commitment is unknown. But in the throes of struggle, the strength of our commitment leaps into sharp focus. Every time our worldly temptations are pitted against our devotion to G-d, the depth of our faith is being tested. In our struggle to overcome our frailties, our bond with Him is strengthened. We unleash the power that lies dormant in our souls; we uncover the depth and strength of our love and our abilities.

This is why G-d planted the tree of forbidden fruit, with all its appeal, in the Garden of Eden. Exposing Adam and Eve to temptation forced them to choose; it pit the allure of the fruit against their love for their Creator. Through this tree, all of humanity was introduced to temptation. Indeed, if not for this tree, we would have lived in spiritual tranquility; we would never be tempted, we would never be challenged, and we would never have to struggle. But we would also never grow. In tempting Adam and Eve, G-d made possible our slide, our descent, from angelic innocence to worldly maturity. In doing so, He also laid the foundation for our ascent from a state of untested faith to enduring strength and commitment.

---

[2] *Bereshit* Rabbah 15:8.

[3] For these questions and their answers, see *Ktav Sofer* on *Genesis* 2:16 and 3:3.

REACHING FOR G-D

Blueberry Muffins

A woman who began keeping kosher later in life told me that her most difficult hurdle was giving up her delicious Boston Blueberry Muffins. I grew up in Boston, ate only kosher food, and never heard of the brand. Today, neither one of us eats these muffins. Yet my restraint is peaceful while hers involves a constant struggle. For the same reason, her struggle continually strengthens her bond with G-d; my restraint is less significant. This form of inner struggle is the legacy that Adam and Eve left us. It is their curse, but also their gift. Every time we encounter a difficult choice, we face the risk of backsliding — but also the opportunity to climb higher.

Without risk, there is no gain. Without gain, there is no achievement. Without achievement, there is no joy. Therefore, G-d created us and our temptations. He would not have created our temptations if they did not benefit us in some way. Every slide downward is an opportunity to climb who-knows-how-many times higher.

"But how do I turn my downward slides into climbing opportunities? How do I overcome my temptations?"

Gaining Dominance
Servants And Masters

After the Flood, when Noah exited the Ark, he planted a vineyard, produced wine, drank his fill and fell into a deep slumber. Ham saw his father lying naked and informed his brothers, whereupon the brothers covered their father's nakedness. When Noah awoke he cursed Ham and damned him to eternal servitude to his righteous brothers.[1]

Ham, who used his eye to see his father's nakedness and his mouth to gossip about it, symbolizes temptations of sight and sound. His brothers, who behaved correctly and restored their father's dignity, symbolize righteousness. Noah, who understood that Ham was a slave to temptation, enslaved Ham to his brothers so that righteousness would rule over temptation.[2]

We often fall prey to desires that are triggered by the sights we see. We are often tempted to speak in ways we know we shouldn't. Tempted though we may be, we're not shackled to these desires. We are able to master them if we only choose to. We have it within our power to draft the powers of sight and speech into the service of righteousness.

Nevertheless, there are times when the servant gains dominance over its master. Where righteousness should master, temptations prevail.[3] These are times when we feel compelled to indulge in those sins that we lust after, when we feel we can't deny ourselves the temptations of which we have caught a fleeting glimpse, when we feel we can't refrain from sharing a deli-

---

[1] *Genesis 9:20–23.*

[2] See Rabbeinu Bachya on *Exodus 21:26.*

[3] Where the heart should rule over the eye, sometimes the eye rules over the heart. As our Sages said, *"The eye sees and the heart desires."* See *Jerusalem Talmud, Berachos* 1:5.

cious piece of gossip or an enjoyable morsel of slander that we accidentally overheard.

It was about this weakness that the prophet Jeremiah lamented, "The servants hold rule over us and we find no rescue."[4] When the servants — our temptations — take over and hold rule over the master, the master must strike back and incapacitate the ability of the eye and ear to tempt us. How is this done?

There are two paths: The first is short but long, the second is long but short.

Short But Long
The short but long path is to implement a full alert and impose regular vigilance over what we see and hear. This path is short because the problem is immediately solved. But it is also long because the remedy lasts only as long as we are motivated. When our vigilance slacks off, the problem resurfaces and we need to start again. This makes for a long journey.

Long But Short
The second path calls for a full internal audit of our spiritual well-being. Why is the heart tempted to those things that are only of temporal value? Why are we enamored by sights and sounds that are stimulating on the surface but devoid of meaning? Why does the heart not grow excited over the opportunity to immerse itself in Torah study? Why does the heart not skip a beat when we approach G-d in prayer? Why are we not as tempted to help the elderly lady to cross the street as we are by all manner of licentious pleasure? Why do we care so much about ourselves and not enough about G-d?

The answer is that we don't devote enough thought to G-d.

Let us pause for a moment and reflect on the fact that G-d created our world and filled it with all manner of things that distract us from our calling. He then created us and placed us among these distractions for a predetermined

---

[4] Eichah 5:8. See also Eichah Rabbah, ibid. and Pirkei D' Rabbi Eliezer 23 and 24.

number of years. During this time, we can choose either to lay the foundation for our eternal edifice, the exquisite pleasures and Divine ecstasy that
await us in the World to Come, or to distract ourselves with all manner of
temporal pleasures. These pleasures will stimulate us for the short duration
of our stay, but when we reach the Next World, we will find ourselves devoid of all merit and unable to partake of its eternal pleasures.

At that time, we will question the decisions we made in This World. Was that
delicious, but non-kosher ice cream worth the price? Was the temporary
pleasure of sharing a morsel of gossip worth the price? We gained twenty
minutes of pleasure, but lost an eternal mitzvah. If we choose to ignore the
gossip and the non-kosher food, it will cost us a few moments of frustration,
but we will earn eternal merit in the World to Come. When we stand before
G-d and are asked to justify our choices, we will want to be proud of the
choices we made.

This path is long but short. It takes a long time to adjust to this point of view.
It is not easy to live by these values. But it is ultimately the short path. Once
we choose it, we need never worry about temptation again. How can one be
tempted by weak, temporal pleasures when exquisite delight awaits us for
eternity?

Such reflection robs the temptation of its appeal and renders it almost entirely impotent.[5]

Who is truly free? Those who master themselves.

---

[5] Loosely based on Commentary of B'er Mayim Chayim on Exodus 21:26–27.

REACHING FOR G-D

"I've tried to follow these ideas, and have embraced my struggle. Actually, I've been experiencing a modicum of success. But when do I get to relax?"

IN CONSTANT FEAR

JACOB WAS WORRIED

No one likes to worry. If we could do away with worry, we would; it serves only to weaken and distract. This does not mean that there's never anything to worry about. We all agree that certain circumstances are indeed worrisome. Jacob also encountered such circumstances: His brother, Esau, wanted to kill him. Jacob was forced to flee from home to escape his brother's wrath.

Many years later, when he finally returned, Jacob's dreaded moment arrived: it was time to confront Esau, who was approaching with a band of four hundred men. Standing there with his entire family, Jacob was indeed worried, and prepared for the worst. If one could find a moment when it was appropriate to worry, this would be it. The Torah relates that "Jacob grew frightened and distressed"; he prayed for deliverance from his brother's hand.[1]

WHAT ABOUT THE PROMISE?

Let us pause and reflect on what worried Jacob. At first glance, the answer seems obvious. His brother was a dangerous man, with a chip on his shoulder, and accompanied by a powerful army. Yet Jacob had one very good reason not to be concerned: an explicit promise from G-d.

On Jacob's leaving his father's house, G-d had appeared to him and declared, "Behold, I am with you, and I will guard you wherever you go, and I will restore you to this Land. For I will not forsake you, until I have done what I have spoken concerning you."[2] When Jacob prepared to return home, G-d reiterated this promise. Jacob had reason to be cautious, going into this predicament with Esau, but he had no cause to be frightened. Knowing that G-d

---

[1] Genesis 32:6.

[2] *Genesis* 28:15 and 31:13. See *Rashi*, ibid. See also *Bereishit Rabbah* 65:19.

would protect him, he should have been confident. Did his worry betray a lack of trust in G-d? Had he forgotten G-d's promise?

JACOB'S WORDS

Jacob himself provides the answer in the words of his famous prayer. Before asking G-d to save him, he declared: "I have become small, from all the kindness and truth You have done for Your servant. For I crossed the Jordan with [only] my walking stick, and now I am the master of two camps."[3] Looking at the precise expressions, we detect the root of his fear. G-d had showered him with blessings and Jacob was humbled by the kindness he was shown. He had "become small," and wondered if he deserved it all.

Aside from this kindness, Jacob was humbled by "truth." What is truth, in this context? Our Sages teach us that the word "truth," when it appears in the Torah, often refers to the Torah itself.[4] Jacob was suggesting that something about his adherence to the Torah had humbled him and possibly even compromised G-d's earlier promise to him.

CONSTANT CONCERN

King Solomon declared, *"Ashrei adam mefached tamid"* ("praiseworthy is the man who is perpetually afraid").[5] At first glance, this statement seems puzzling, as it suggests that the anxiety is a virtue. But our Sages explain that the verse refers to a specific context. As mentioned, the word "truth" denotes Torah. The Hebrew word for truth is *"emet."* The Hebrew letters comprising the word *"emet"* form an acronym for the above phrase, *"Ashrei adam mefached tamid."* The verse, therefore, is saying that one must be perpetually concerned about one's personal study of Torah — that regardless of one's accomplishments, one must never assume that one possesses an unassailable mastery over the subject studied, but must constantly review to ensure that the acquired wisdom is not forgotten.

---

[3] *Genesis* 32:11.

[4] Jerusalem Talmud, Rosh Hashanah 3:8.

[5] Proverbs 28:14. See Babylonian Talmud, Brachos 60a.

Jacob understood that protection against his brother's schemes came from the ability to remain in constant contact with all he had learned, to stay focused on retaining the fruits of his spiritual toil. He worried that even a small distraction or interruption might cause him to forget, and eventually neglect, the Torah.

But what could possibly distract a person of his caliber or affect his staunch devotion?

TRIALS OF PROSPERITY

Following the words, "I am humbled by the kindness and truth," Jacob went on to say, " ... For with my stick I crossed the Jordan, and I am now the master of two camps." In this sentence Jacob describes his meteoric rise from poverty to great wealth. What is the link between this verse about wealth and the preceding verse about humility and diligence in Torah study?

The Torah speaks of two situations in which our faith is tested: There is the trial of poverty, when one is forced to struggle desperately to survive, constantly begging G-d for sustenance. This is exceedingly difficult. But there is another trial that is, in some respects, even more crippling than that of poverty. It is the trial of prosperity. The Torah cautions us against growing haughty as our wealth increases. As our collection of gold and silver expands, the Torah exhorts us not to forget G-d, Who redeemed us from Egypt.[6]

Once we experience financial success, we often attribute our success to our own efforts and talents, proclaiming ourselves masters of our own destiny. Blessed with prosperity, many fail to remember their humble origins. They forget those who raised them and invested in them, those who helped them and believed in them. They dismiss those who supported them when they were down and assisted them on their way up. The first "victim" of this forgetfulness is often G-d.

---

[6] Deuteronomy 11:8–18.

THE ULTIMATE TEST

Jacob crossed the Jordan a poor man; all he had was his walking stick. He endured the test of poverty and returned as a man of means, a master of two camps. But he was not pleased. He would have been happier without his wealth, for he understood that prosperity is a difficult test. His faith, his conviction, his absolute commitment to the Torah was now being tried, and he felt vulnerable. He worried that his wealth might have distracted him from Torah study, leading him to forget or possibly even neglect that which he had studied. He now had cause to be frightened. Neglecting the Torah would strip him of his father's blessing and leave him vulnerable to his brother's attack.

When their mother, Rebecca, had been pregnant with twins she had consulted a prophet about the future of her children. The prophet informed her, "Two nations are in your womb; two regimes shall separate from your womb. Might shall pass from one regime to the other."[7] Power passes back and forth between Jacob and Esau. When Jacob is loyal to the Torah, he is in the ascendency; when Jacob betrays the Torah, Esau rises to power. Jacob knew that should he fail his test of prosperity he would become vulnerable to his brother, Esau. He therefore appealed to G-d for salvation.

Jacob's fear was not born of lack of faith. On the contrary, it was in the spirit of King Solomon's teaching that Jacob grew frightened. His worry demonstrated that he *had* passed the test of wealth; rather than turning from G-d, he sought with all his heart to remain connected to G-d. G-d heard his prayer and granted his desire. When Jacob finally met Esau, he was greeted with love rather than hatred.

Jacob's attitude is one we should try to model. Irrespective of our past achievements, we are all subject to the frailties of human nature. We cannot rest complacent with the successes of our past, because our past does not secure our future. Our commitment today does not ensure our commitment

---

[7] *Genesis* 25:23. See *Rashi*, ibid. See also *Bereishit Rabbah* 65:19.

REACHING FOR G-D

tomorrow. We must never let down our guard.[8] In the face of Torah, in the face of "truth," we recall the acronym, *"Ashrei adam mefached tamid."* Like Jacob, we must remain humble.[9]

Our past failures cannot destroy our future. Our past successes cannot ensure our future. The choice about our future is in our hands.

---

[8] Struggling to overcome our weaknesses is also a form of Divine worship. Success is not necessarily defined by reaching a state in which we no longer need to struggle. Constant struggle is also a form of success. G-d expects according to our ability. The average person (who is not endowed with the soul of a Tzadik) is incapable of winning the internal war and G-d does not expect this of us. G-d does expect us to maintain a continual struggle regardless of past failures and when we do so we are regarded as His perfect servants. See Tanya ch. 27.

[9] This essay is based on commentary from *Divrei Yisrael* on *Genesis* 32:13.

"But the task seems so daunting! Am I really capable of winning this struggle?"

THE RAINMAKER
RAIN AND DEW

When on vacation, I like to rise early to pray, study, and enjoy the crisp ambiance of an early summer morning. Some mornings, I awake to the patter of rainfall as a soft drizzle sprinkles the ground and cools the air. Other mornings, I awake to glorious sunshine, the grass covered by shimmering dew that glistens like a million stars.

Both mornings are wet — one with rain and the other with dew — yet they evoke very different responses. One is gentle and soothing; the other is cheerful and invigorating. The difference is usually attributed to the sunlight or lack thereof, but spiritually speaking, the difference can be attributed to the nature of the moisture itself: the rain or the dew.

Before his passing, Moses gave his final testament. As introduction, he composed a song of praise, a composition of lilting poetry. "May the heavens listen as I speak, and may the earth hearken to my words! May my teaching flow like rain, and may my words drip like dew!"[1]

Noting the two similes that Moses employed — rain and dew — the Midrash offers the following homily: "Israel requested that their inspiration flow like rain. To which G-d replied, 'No, not like rain. Better that it should drip like dew.'" Israel wanted rain, but G-d wanted dew. Both are condensed vapor; both are moist, and visible on the ground. What is the difference?

THE ORIGIN

The difference is in their origin. Rain is formed when moisture from below evaporates and rises into the atmosphere, where it condenses, forms clouds, and precipitates as rain. Dew does not require rising vapors; dew is formed here on earth, when the temperature cools and the warmer vapors contact

---

[1] Deuteronomy 32:2.

the cooler surface. The rain cycle begins with an ascent from below: the cycle of dew requires no ascent.

To understand the importance of this distinction, and its relevance to Moses' request and the Divine response, we must first understand the spiritual parallel.

RISING FROM BELOW

Just as evaporated waters rise from the surface below to the skies above, so do we. Like the ocean waters, we are generally content with life here below, where we are spiritually distant from G-d. Tossed about on waves of whim, we often focus on the body rather than the soul, on the material and physical rather than the spiritual. But, like the ocean waters, our contentment cannot last forever. Eventually, we too feel the need to ascend.

During the High Holy Days, our minds turn to G-d. We remember our spiritual void. We realize that we live in a morally bankrupt society, where conceit and arrogance, selfishness and rage, permissiveness and corruption are common. With this realization, we pine for a more meaningful existence; our material lifestyle loses its allure. Our enthusiasm for it evaporates. And, like evaporated moisture over the oceans, we rise to a higher, more spiritual plane.

From this vantage point, we look back with dismay and form clouds of remorse in the higher atmosphere. These clouds obstruct the light, replacing our cheer with shame. But these clouds must not be permitted to linger. Beads of inspiration must soon form within our hearts, beads that will precipitate a torrential outpouring of love for G-d, and inspire us to study the Torah and observe its *mitzvot*.

MOSES AND G-D

Understanding the fickle nature of mankind, Moses knew that few people can maintain a constant level of devotion. Moses therefore asked that G-d make our inspiration flow like rain. Like raindrops that form from evaporated waters below, so did Moses ask G-d to accept our penitence from the lower plane. This would, in turn, lift us to a higher plane and precipitate within us an outpouring of love for G-d.

G-d replied that, instead, inspiration would drip, like dew. Dew forms on the surface below and does not require its vapors to rise. G-d was saying that He would work to inspire our souls, independently of the choices we make. When G-d sees that we stray from the path of Torah, He does not wait for our spiritual vapors to rise; He does not wait for us to repent. He proactively plants a bead of inspiration within our souls, and stimulates within us the desire for a mitzvah.

SPONTANEOUS DESIRES

Sometimes we read something or hear something that inspires us. But other times, we are consumed by an inexplicable desire to do something good — to attend services at the synagogue, to light Shabbat candles, or donate money to charity. These desires appear spontaneously; they are not stimulated by anything we have seen or heard. They are dew-like inspirations, stimulated by G-d, not by our ascent from below.

G-d stimulates the desire, but leaves the implementation to us. We have a choice: we can either confine ourselves to experiencing and acting on a single inspiration, or we can use this inspiration to stimulate further inspiration for additional *mitzvot*. In other words, we can either make rain or wait for the next dew. Let us choose rain.[2]

Beads of inspiration come and go. Whether they will influence us, and how, is up to us. Moses taught that G-d is helping us, and that He endows us with the spiritual endurance to persevere and ultimately to triumph.

---

[2] This essay is based on Likutei Torah, p. 73b.

REACHING FOR G-D

"I hear that G-d sends me beads of inspiration. But what do I do if despite my best efforts I cannot make those beads last? My soul keeps trying, but my temptations keep winning."

BLESSINGS FROM ABOVE
THE WAYWARD SON
He was a glutton for meat, drank alcohol to excess, and disobeyed his parents at every turn. He mocked their pleas and their discipline and refused to accept their instruction. Instead, he sought to instruct his parents. He demanded that they pay for his excessive habits, and when they wouldn't, he simply stole what he needed.

Presenting themselves before the *beit din*, his parents declared that their son was a glutton and a drunkard, who refused to obey them. The Torah commands the *beit din* to sentence the son to death.[1]

According to our Sages, such an incident has never occurred in all of Jewish history. Though this law is recorded in the Torah, it is pure hypothesis. Yet we know that the Torah's every word has practical relevance to us and must be instructive in our daily worship of G-d. This incident, too, despite its purely hypothetical nature, must contain a lesson for us. Otherwise, it would not appear in the Torah.[2]

A WAYWARD PEOPLE
According to the Jewish mystics, this passage refers collectively to us, the Jewish People. From the moment of birth we are constantly reminded that we share a special relationship with G-d.[3] We are told that our nation has been singled out for spiritual greatness, that each of us is destined for a life of sanctity, and that we are endowed with a sublime spark of the Divine, a sacred soul that is breathed into us by G-d. We know that by virtue of our soul we are plugged into millennia of Jewish history. We realize that we share a

---

[1] Deuteronomy 21:18. See also commentary of Abarbanel.

[2] Babylonian Talmud, Sanhedrin 71 b.

[3] *Zohar*, Section III, p. 187b.

kinship with the likes of Moses and Abraham. We understand that our destiny is intertwined with those spiritual giants who preceded us. We recognize that their sacrifices and achievements have paved our way and that they watch us with interest to see if we will follow in their footsteps and perpetuate their legacy. We know that if we do, our fleeting lives will leave an indelible mark on eternity.

We know it, yet we often ignore it. We opt for a life of pleasure and ease rather than commitment and sacrifice. We choose comfort over piety, earth over heaven, body over soul. We place our needs ahead of our ancestors' needs, our interests before G-d's. For the price of temporal pleasure, we throw away eternal bliss and our encounter with destiny. Just like the wayward child, who weighs himself down with gluttonous ways and allows his body to dominate his soul, so, too, do we invest in corporeal pleasures and thus allow our soul to be dominated by the desires of our body.[4] Just like the wayward child, we refuse to be guided by our Father in Heaven. He offers instruction, and in return we offer advice. Instead of learning the true meaning of life from the Master of all meaning, we offer suggestions to G-d on how He might best conduct His affairs. We truly do believe that we know better.

THE INTERNAL STRUGGLE
We know where we belong, yet we lack the strength to go there. We know what we desire, yet we lack the courage to reach for it. If the truth be told, we are conflicted. On the one hand, our baser elements drive us to instant gratification and hollow pursuits that strip life of all meaning. On the other hand, our Divine spark yearns for something more profound; it reaches for something greater, and aspires to a more meaningful life.

---

[4] According to Ikarim (3:15), G-d permitted Noah to eat meat, in order to demonstrate man's superiority over animals. However, when man descends to a bestial level, gluttonous meat eating can result in cruelty and a desire for materialism. See Abarbanel on Deuteronomy 12:20.

When we study the story of the wayward child, that supposed abstraction that has never come to life, we realize that we are, in fact, that proverbial son. How do we remove ourselves from this endless quagmire? We follow the steps outlined in the Torah for the wayward child.[5]

THE DIVINE SOLUTION

We stand before G-d and testify that our children refuse to obey us. Who are these children? The Talmud refers to man's actions as his offspring. Children are the offspring of their parents, and our actions are the offspring of our hearts and minds. We attempt to correct our behavior, but are unsuccessful. Our actions betray our best intentions. They do not obey our instruction. They do not hearken to our voices. Our testimony is a heartfelt plea for Divine assistance in overcoming our evil inclination.

G-d generously responds and consigns our offspring, our errant actions, to proverbial death. This means that he gives us the strength to be disciplined, to overcome our baser elements, and to correct our inappropriate behavior. With this Divine assistance, we are empowered to win the match. We are now able to respond to the call of destiny and to take up the torch left for us by our ancestors.[6]

This may be the reason that the Torah tells us of the wayward child. It teaches that to overcome the allure of temporal pleasures, we must seek a blessing from the Divine, an infusion of spiritual strength. We must appear before G-d and acknowledge that we cannot do it alone, that our actions have run amok.

---

[5] See commentary of Be'er Mayim Chayim on Deuteronomy 21:18.

[6] Note that G-d does not command our passions to cease, only our actions. This is because the passions themselves are not forbidden; succumbing to them is. The experience of life as a war between two impulses is normal. It is the way G-d intended it. However, to gain the upper hand in this struggle requires a superhuman effort, an act made possible only by the grace of G-d.

G-d does not demand that which we cannot deliver. When He demands that we improve our behavior and overcome our weaknesses and cravings, He also empowers us to do so. The order itself is empowering. The demand itself is a blessing — a blessing that has the power to extract us from an otherwise hopeless and endless quagmire.

THE REWARD

This may explain the rabbinic dictum that the purely hypothetical Torah portion about the wayward child was written only so that we might learn it and receive reward. This Torah portion orders us to improve, indeed empowers us to improve. When we learn this portion, we are rewarded with this Divine power, which is indeed a worthwhile reward.[7]

The road to piety is lifelong. But if we are determined to reach our destiny, G-d will see to it that we do.

---

[7] The reward aspect is explained also in the commentary of Maharshah to *Sanhedrin* 71a. See also commentary of Kli Yakar on *Deuteronomy* 21:18.

"I find that life in this world is filled with distractions, everywhere I turn. How do we remember the Heaven's beauty when we are distracted here on earth?

TRAVEL BEGINS AND ENDS AT HOME

TRUE BEAUTY IS WITHIN

Listening to the car radio, on my way home from a particularly long trip, I heard an accomplished, world-famous traveler declare that her most amazing life experiences had been accomplished within the confines of her own house. She had made the most wondrous observations in the privacy of her own home.

Here was a woman who had toured the world again and again, on a quest for meaning and fulfillment. She had traveled far and wide on many a journey of discovery, and experienced the global perspectives of multiple cultures and faiths. She had taken in the sights, smells, and tastes of exotic, faraway lands. But to her amazement, she discovered that there is no discovery like the self-discovery that takes place in our own home.

She discovered that true beauty, meaning, and truth cannot be found in distant lands, unless one has first discovered it within. She also discovered that once beauty is discovered within, travel no longer beckons. Because the beauty we find within our lives and ourselves is far more satisfying than the beauty that lies outside of us.

TRUE TREASURES ARE AT HOME

When I heard her saying this, I reflected on how mankind is never content. An inner force drives us to reach out and seek greater beauty, to venture forth in pursuit of greater knowledge, to explore new frontiers, and to scale new heights. We spend billions of dollars on exploring outer space. We expend tremendous energy in our attempt to decipher the genetic code. From the microscopic to the macroscopic, we are constantly driven to explore the secrets of heaven and earth.

The story is told of a poor, pious Jew in Krackow, who dreamed that there was a treasure to be found under the great bridge in Prague. He woke up, and traveled to that far-off bridge. But when he started to dig, he was immediately stopped by a police officer. When the man told the officer about his dream, the policeman broke out in raucous laughter. "You trust dreams?!" he asked incredulously. "Why, just last night, I dreamed that there is a treasure awaiting me under the floorboards of a home in Krackow!" And then, to this fellow's astonishment, the policeman mentioned his own address! He hurried home, and found the treasure.

How ironic! That man had traveled such a great distance in pursuit of a treasure that, all along, was waiting for him in his own home.

We too expend so much energy traveling the world, exploring its secrets, and studying its nature — all in a quest for meaning and beauty. We work so hard to find the beauty of our universe, but the truth is that there is even greater beauty within us. For in every human being is concealed a piece of Heaven.

Bringing Heaven Down to Earth

A human being is an amalgam of body and soul. Heaven and earth join forces to make up the composite that is man. The force of the material weighs us down. We are, by our material nature, responsive to the material pleasures of earth; its delights entice us and distract us from our spiritual goals. However, despite its endless attraction, we are left unsatisfied. The beauty of nature inspires and delights us spiritually. But even this continual delight and inspiration leave us yearning for something more.

Earth's beauty inspires and delights our souls because it is a reflection, a glimpse, of our inner, Heavenly beauty. But we are still left yearning for something more, because it is only a glimpse. The earthly plane is only a shadow of the true beauty and meaning in Heaven. A piece of Heaven is contained within us we are subconsciously familiar with its beauty. We cannot envision it in our minds, but we know enough to recognize when something pales by comparison. Thus, when we plug into earthly beauty we sense that we are only tantalizing ourselves, for there is so much more beauty to behold.

Why, then, do we not immediately turn inward for the truest form of beauty? Why do we waste our time with the partial and flawed rendition? Because plugging into beauty on earth is easy, almost effortless, whereas plugging into our inner, Heavenly beauty is laborious, a constant challenge.

We each have a latent, G-d-given ability to bring Heaven's beauty down to earth.[1] But making that choice is difficult.[2] The great Rebbe Levi Yitzchok of Berditchev is reputed to have complained to G-d: "You have placed the temptation of the material before our eyes, but concealed the desire for Yourself within Your Book [the Torah]. Could You not have reversed this, and thus made it a little easier for us?"

DREAMING OF HEAVEN AND EARTH
The Torah speaks of Joseph's two dreams. In one dream, he and his brothers were gathering sheaves of wheat in the field; the brothers' sheaves suddenly

---

[1] Every moment presents a choice of Heaven or earth. We can take the easy route and make it a moment of earth, or the laborious route and make it a moment of Heaven. Every breath we take, every drop we drink, every bite we eat can be consumed for the purpose of sustaining the body alone, or also for sustaining the soul. It is easy to think only of material needs; the challenge is to bring Heaven down to earth, by focusing on spirituality as the goal. For more information, see Tanya, ch. 7.

[2] As a young child, the former Rebbe of Lubavitch asked his father to help him understand the unique nature of the Jew. His father summoned the simple servant who had served the family for many years. "Ben Tzion," he asked. "Why do you eat in the morning?" "I eat so that I can live," replied Ben Tzion. "And why must you live?" asked the father. "I must live so that I can pray to G-d, study Torah, and fulfill His commandments," replied Ben Tzion. "You see," concluded the father. "This is a Jew. Everyone eats in order to live. But why does a Jew want to live? A Jew lives for G-d." Everyone needs to sustain his body. But only a person who has nurtured his soul knows that the body is an instrument of the soul. (Likutei Diburim, p. 421)

bowed to Joseph's sheaf. In the second dream, eleven stars, the sun, and the moon bowed to Joseph's star.[3] These dreams were similar in content but not in context. The first dream occurred on earth, while the second dream occurred in the heavens.

Pharaoh also had two dreams. In one dream, seven emaciated cows consumed seven healthy cows. In the second dream, seven healthy stalks absorbed seven dried-out stalks.[4] Both of Pharaoh's dreams occurred on earth.

Why is it that Joseph's dreams ascended from earth to Heaven, but Pharaoh's dreams remained on earth?

In Joseph's first dream, everyone engaged in the laborious task of bundling sheaves in the field, under the hot sun. Difficult work, but one who is prepared to work hard is capable of climbing the ladder to Heaven. One who chooses not to take on this hardship remains, like Pharaoh, forever earthbound.[5]

Not for us, descendants of Joseph, is the facile and effortless way. G-d did not put us in this world to enjoy the easy life. We are here to make the difficult choices; to make the arduous climb and to bring Heaven down to earth. That is what makes us special; that is what makes us the Chosen People.

When the grass seems greener on the other side of the fence, it's good to remember that, really, the grass is greenest right where we

---

[3] That the first dream occurred on earth and the second dream occurred in the heaven is noteworthy. As soon as we are born into the material world the enticements begin. Our *yetzer hara* (evil inclination) is in full force, from the moment we are born. The *yetzer tov* (heavenly inclination) isn't in full force until the age of bar/bat mitzvah. That happens later, which is why the heavenly dream came second. See *Bereishit Rabbah*, ch. 53. See also Zohar, vol. 2, 98.

[4] Genesis 41: 1-7.

[5] See Likutei Sichot, vol. III, p. 807.

are. Overcoming the distraction of the other side is not always easy, but when we do we are treated to a glimpse of true beauty.

"Plugging into Heaven's beauty by immersing ourselves into a life of seclusion and Torah study sounds lovely. Is that our mandate?"

ON REMOVING SHOES
HEAVEN AND EARTH

A road among the steep mountains just outside Premishlan was impassable during the winter, due to treacherous, icy conditions. Yet the Chassidic master Rebbe Meir of Premishlan would navigate it regularly. When asked his secret, he answered simply, "One who's attached Above doesn't fall below."

Harnessing the power of Heaven to enhance the quality of earth has always been a Jewish goal. When Moses led a flock of sheep across the desert, and from there to G-d's mountain, this was on his mind.[1] He herded his sheep across the desert and contemplated the parallels between his current flock and the nation that he would one day lead across that very terrain.[2] Because of its docile character and gentle temperament, the sheep is symbolic of humility.[3] The Jewish mandate at Sinai would be to subject themselves to G-d in absolute humility.[4]

The Jew would be asked to function on earth, but to engage the heavens. *Is it possible to bridge the two?* Moses mused. *Will the Jew survive here on earth, and successfully resist the pull of Heaven?* As he gazed out on the desert, Moses marveled at the paradox involved in uniting the two opposite forces. The desert, Moses prophetically knew, was where humanity would receive its

---

[1] *Exodus* 3:1–5.

[2] Zohar, Exodus 21a.

[3] *Midrash Shir Hashirim* 2:17a. The *midrash* enumerates many comparisons of our relationship with G-d — such as father and son, shepherd and sheep (as it is written, "And I shall place my sheep, the sheep of my flock" [*Ezekiel* 34]). For the difference in meaning between the two, see Ohr Hatorah, p. 755, and Likutei Sichot, vol. 15, p. 2–53.

[4] Likutei Torah Leviticus, p. 37.

first glimpse of Jewish greatness.[5] The desert, Moses realized, was where Jews would first encounter G-d. And then he understood: It would be this encounter with G-d that would empower Jews to bring the heavens down to earth.[6]

AN EXPERIENCE ON THE MOUNTAIN

Moses set out on a journey of discovery, across the desert, exploring one spiritual frontier after another.[7] He found himself drawn to G-d's mountain, as iron is drawn to a magnet. This, he knew, was where Heaven and earth would meet, where G-d would descend and the human ascend.[8] He approached the mountain with great awe, and beheld a fascinating sight. A thorn-bush was engulfed in flames, yet the bush was not consumed. [9]

In his contemplation, Moses immediately grasped the meaning behind the vision. The fire was symbolic of the Jews' smoldering passion for G-d; it rages within our hearts, but doesn't consume us.[10] Moses was mesmerized. *Why*

---

[5] *Shemot Rabbah* 2:4. The *midrash* explains that Moses was drawn to the desert because of all the great miracles — the manna, the Clouds of Glory, and others — that would be performed on behalf of the Jewish People in the desert.

[6] *Shemot Rabbah* 2:2 relates that Moses chased a sheep that ran for many miles. When the sheep finally reached water, Moses cried out, *"Had I only known that you were thirsty, I would have brought the water myself!"* And he carried the sheep back. When G-d saw this, He proclaimed that Moses, who knew how to care for the needs of each individual, was worthy of being a shepherd to the Jewish People. This story may also be understood allegorically. The sheep is Israel, and the water is the Torah. Moses chased the sheep to find out what drives it and discovered that Torah is the source of its nourishment. When he saw this, he carried the nation in his arms and brought the Torah to them.

[7] See Rabbeinu Bachya on this verse.

[8] See note 2 above.

[9] See note 1 above.

[10] The classic understanding of the metaphor is that the bush is Israel and the flames are its persecutors. Despite the intensity of its persecutions, Israel will never be consumed. Alternatively, the bush is Egypt and the flames are the Ten Plagues. Despite the intensity of the plagues, Egypt would survive to absorb eve-

will the bush not burn? he wondered.[11] *Why does the pull of Heaven not consume the Jew?*

Moses sought to broaden his meditative experience, and reached to attain the prophetic plateau.[12] To achieve this transcendental perspective, he knew he would have to transcend his own ego and behold the vision in a different way.[13] He quietly murmured, "I shall turn from here, so as to behold this great vision." In other words, I shall turn away from my own ego, in an effort to behold this great vision.[14] The earlier vision now leaped into sharper focus. Moses now perceived an angel dancing amid the flames and summoning him to the bush.

He was seized by a sudden impulse to rush forward, to abandon everything and luxuriate in G-d's beatific Presence.[15] "*Here am I!*" he exclaimed.[16] At that moment, G-d appeared and sternly instructed, "Do not draw closer. Remove your shoes from your feet. For the ground you stand on is holy."[17] G-d did

---

ry last one of them. See *Shemot Rabbah* 2:5 and Kli Yakar. But the interpretation in this essay follows commentary from Rabbeinu Bachya on this verse.

[11] See note 1 above.

[12] *Shemot Rabbah* 2:5. At first, an intermediary angel descended. Then the *Shechinah* itself descended. See also Rabbeinu Bachya, Ramban, and Malbim.

[13] Maimonides' *Yesodei Hatorah*, ch. 7. Taam Vadaat offers a unique view of the instruction to Moses to remove his shoes. He explains that shoes lift a person up off the ground and are symbolic of arrogance. Moses was told to strengthen his humility.

[14] The Hebrew word is "*asurah.*" Most commentators translate this word as "I shall turn [towards the fire]," meaning "I shall draw closer to the fire." The interpretation in this essay relies on commentary from Kli Yakar on this verse and that of Kedushat Levi.

[15] *Shemot Rabbah* 2:6.

[16] See note 1 above.

[17] See note 1 above.

not grant him permission to tread there, because he was not yet ready. [18]

ONE RESPONSE, TWO MEANINGS

G-d's response was not given in reproof, but in guidance — not only to Moses but also to us, across the generations. The Jewish experience is suspended between Heaven and earth. To inherit it, we must enhance both dimensions within us, that of Heaven and that of earth. How? In both cases we must remove our shoes. [19]

Shoes are outer garments that conceal our feet as they tread on the earth. They are symbolic of the body, which is also a garment, that dresses the soul in a cloak of materialism as it sojourns here on earth.[20]

To ascend G-d's mountain, to enhance our spirit, we must remove our shoes, our materialism. Materialism is appropriate in a material milieu; but on G-d's mountain, it is a hindrance. There we must divest ourselves of material considerations and be fully devoted to a holy existence.[21]

---

[18] See Ramban on this verse. He writes that Moses had not yet reached the pinnacle of the prophecy that he would attain on his return to Sinai and when leading the Jewish nation.

[19] This section of the discussion is predicated on two contrary interpretations of Moses's shoes. The classic meaning is the one first depicted here. The second, and opposite, reading is based on Kedushat Levi on this verse.

[20] See commentaries from Malbim and Kli Yakar. Rabbeinu Bachya adds that the shoe itself is symbolic of materialism. He says that materialism clings to the body as the shoe molds to the foot.

These commentaries add that when a man refuses to marry his brother's childless widow, his shoe must be removed in the *chalitzah* ceremony. The symbolism therein is that since he refused to establish a material heir to his brother's lineage, his shoe must be removed.

[21] Rabbeinu Bachya sees the Hebrew word *"shal"* as being from the root word *"shlilah,"* which means "negation." Hence the words "remove your shoes" read as "negate your materialism."

Once we climb the mountain and reach the summit, descent seems unappealing. From the peak of G-d's mountain, the material realm loses its appeal. We prefer to float in the heavens above and never return to earth below. Camping out on the peak is tempting. But G-d wants us to descend. G-d wants us to reengage our materialism. And in a way, this means that we must, once again, remove our shoes.

The view we have discussed till now has been that shoes are the garment of materialism, and that by removing them, Moses disengaged from his own materialism. In contradistinction to this view, there are those who argue that, by removing his shoes, Moses actually *engaged* his materialism. [22] This interpretation views shoes as flotation devices that serve to cushion our feet from the material ground. Metaphorically speaking, they shield us from our own materialism. Accordingly, shoes must be worn when we climb G-d's mountain and move away from our materialism, but they must be removed when we descend the mountain to reengage the material world.

We reengage the material world because only in this world is it possible to serve the Divine mandate. It is G-d's wish that we share the insights and inspiration that we have gleaned at the top of the mountain with those who have yet to make the climb. This Divine wish can be fulfilled only at the base of the mountain; among the foothill dwellers. We cannot fulfill this wish while remaining separated from the earth where this wish must be fulfilled.

Shemot Rabbah (6:7) suggests that Moses asked that his family become the royal family of Israel, but he was refused. Kedushat Levi explains that a king must connect with the nation to exert a positive influence. Moses's thoughts were perpetually locked in the celestial sphere and focused on G-d, which made him unfit for kingship. Nevertheless, he was king over the generation in the desert, since they, too, were primarily focused on the study of Torah and spiritual pursuit. In this sense, Kedushat Levi sees the Hebrew word *"na'al,"* "shoe," from the root word *"ne'ilah,"* which means "locked" and the Hebrew word *"raglecha,"* from the Hebrew root *"regilut,"* which means "habit" or "routine." The instruction would thus read, "Remove the lock that habitually fixes your thoughts on the Divine, and pay more attention to the people."

The material ground we tread on is thus hallowed and we don't want our shoes to separate us from our hallowed materialism. We must remove our shoes. [23]

Our mission is not to escape to a place that mirrors Heaven. Our mission is to link Heaven and earth. Thus, the foothills of G-d's holy mountain are even holier than its peak.

This is the mystical reason for the Jewish Exile into foreign lands. G-d scattered His children to the lowest of the lowlands, knowing that in Exile, the Jew would uplift his environment and make it holy. The further away from the Land of Israel we are sent, the more we manifest the truth that the foot of the mountain is even holier than its peak. See Sfat Emet 5685.

"Life on earth seems so spiritually barren! If linking Heaven and earth is indeed our purpose — how is this to be done?"

Do Jews Dig Wells?
The Thrill of Discovery

Many of the biblical narratives seem like ancient history, with no particular relevance to our lives. But it is often in the details of these narratives that the most profound and relevant messages are to be found. The story of Isaac and his well-digging is one such example.

Granted, we do not think too much about wells these days, but let's imagine what such a project entails: You need water, and begin digging in a spot where you believe there is a water source. You dig for days, but with no success. You start to wonder if you should give up, or perhaps dig deeper. You keep trying, and are finally rewarded with a fresh wellspring. Pure water suddenly abounds. Your efforts were not in vain. Imagine the thrill! You doubted the purpose, the meaning, of your labor, but now your discovery has proven that your efforts were worthwhile. Your continual toil has been granted the dignity of purpose, of meaning.

Digging for Life's Purpose

A well-digger is a person with a vision. Most people see the desert as a barren, lifeless space, but the well-digger sees it differently. He looks at the dry rocks and hard soil and pictures the hidden wellspring that flows beneath. Though there is no evidence of water and no guarantee that this situation will change, he digs and explores anyway. After great labor, he meets with success. The enormous wellspring that he discovers transforms the entire landscape. What was once barren is now beautiful — an oasis, shaded by trees, adorned with grass and flowers, brought to life by water, the elixir of life.

Most people are content to remain occupied with surface endeavors in life. They see the quest to uncover meaning as a futile pursuit. But the Torah reminds us that a Jew must see things differently. Our Patriarchs were avid well-diggers, and the wells they dug paved the way for our personal progress.[1] The wells they dug in the desert were symbolic of the wells that we must dig within our souls.

We begin with a view of life that is tinged with the mundane, but we persist in the belief that there must be more to life than that which is visible on the surface. We examine our mundane activities and seek out their potential for Divine purpose. We toil, till we finally discover the infinite wellsprings of G-dliness that lie beneath the surface. With this discovery, our life is transformed. We move from a meaningless pursuit of selfish pleasures toward a life where all activities are endowed with infinite meaning.

THE DIVINE AGENDA

We eat and drink, work and play, read and relax. But to what end? Every action has an underlying motivation that serves a Divine purpose. On the surface, we work to earn money to provide for ourselves and our families. On a more refined level, our purpose must be to fulfill the mitzvah of giving charity. Likewise, we can eat to enjoy the taste of a good meal, or we can eat with a higher end in mind — so that we can be nourished and live. The ultimate goal is to realize that the purpose of living is to connect to G-d. Thus, instead of trivializing the physical act of eating, we discover that eating itself is a service to G-d. When we ensure that the food is kosher and recite the proper blessings before and after we eat, we connect our most mundane activities with our most meaningful purpose.

Every activity can be subjected to such rigorous analysis. Let's consider the example of buying and caring for a car. We own a car so that we can drive, but how does driving serve G-d? On the surface, it is difficult to conceive of a Divine purpose to driving a car, but when we search beneath the surface we find meaning in this, too. When we offer someone a ride, we fulfill the mitzvah of loving our fellow man. Thus, we serve a purpose greater than ourselves. The time and effort we expend in beautifying our car enhances the experience of the passenger. We thought we were cleaning the car for our-

---

[1] *Genesis* 26:15–22.

selves, but now we discover that it was for the purpose of enhancing our mitzvah.

We can similarly examine every detail of our daily routine and discover the wellsprings in every moment that endow life with meaning. An action previously seen as dull is now filled with purpose and meaning. What was previously insignificant or habitual has now become G-dly.

UNCAPPING PLUGGED WELLS

There is yet another lesson we can learn from our Patriarchs' well-digging. Abraham dug many wells, but, after Abraham's passing, these wells were stopped up by the Philistines. The Philistines were attracted to the material world, and resisted Abraham's message of spiritual enlightenment. It is because they resisted the influence of Abraham's *spiritual* wells that they labored to stop up his *physical* wells.

At first, they appeared to have succeeded. But along came Isaac, Abraham's son, to ensure that his father's efforts had not been in vain. Isaac, who learned the art of well-digging from Abraham, reopened his father's wells and dug many wells of his own.

We too often experience the frustration of having our "wells stopped up" by our attraction to the material. Every morning, we devote our earliest waking hours to prayer and meditation. Gripped by the fervor of sacred devotion, we resolve to seek the Divine purpose in every endeavor. Uplifted by a wave of inspiration, we discover the well within our souls.

Yet, as we see from the story of Abraham, wells can become blocked and focused strength is needed to unblock them. We step out into the street, and gradually revert to old habits. The wellsprings opened through the morning's prayer can be stopped up by the demanding pursuit of material affairs, and we must find a way to reopen them.

ISAAC'S DISCIPLINE

What are the tools used for opening these wells? Love for G-d is a powerful tool to open the well inside, but love alone does not guarantee that the well will stay open. Abraham, who served G-d out of love, discovered many wellsprings. Yet, after his passing, the Philistines managed to block these wells. Another element was needed.

Isaac, who exemplified the quality of discipline, added the extra force needed to ensure that the wells stay open.[2].

The passion of prayer uncaps the morning's wellsprings — and for that we thank Abraham. But when the prayer ends and the passionate outpouring of love subsides, we must activate our inner resolve to have the discipline to keep our wellsprings flowing throughout the day. Discipline and steadfast loyalty keep temptation at bay and ensure that the waters keep flowing.

And for that, we thank Isaac. [3]

Heavenly gems are embedded within every earthly activity. Uncovering these gems is the process of linking Heaven and earth. Neither Abraham nor Isaac could have done it alone. But together, they created our formula for each day's spiritual success.

---

[2] See Nachmanides's commentary, ibid., that the three wells dug by Isaac were portents of the three Temples — the first two, that were built and destroyed; and the third that will be built in the Messianic era and stand forever. (This is why the first two wells were contested by the Philistines and the third was not.) The purpose of digging the wells was to reveal G-dly purpose in life. Since this G-dly purpose will be fully revealed in the Messianic era, Isaac stopped digging after he discovered the third well.

[3] This essay is based on Sfat Emet 5633

The process of bringing holiness to the mundane and Heaven to earth sounds beautiful. But it was started by our exalted ancestors, many millennia ago. Where do I fit in?"

THE POWER TO UPLIFT

TORAH IN CHINESE

Thirty-seven days before his passing, Moses set out to teach the Torah. We might think that Moses would use his remaining weeks to teach hitherto un-revealed mysteries, but this was not the case. Instead, he translated the Torah into seventy languages.[1] All this for a People who did not even speak these languages.

Have you ever attended a service in a language you did not understand? I have, and it left me uninspired. Why did Moses teach the Torah in languages that his students didn't understand?

This question should actually be asked of G-d. The Talmud teaches that G-d uttered the Ten Commandments in seventy languages, though only the version in the Holy Tongue, Ancient Hebrew, was heard. What was the point of speaking in languages that no one heard, let alone understood?[2]

These questions are compounded when we consider that the written Torah includes several words in Aramaic, Greek, Kapti, and Afriki — languages probably unknown to Jews of that time.[3]

TALMUD IN ARAMAIC

One can argue that translating the Torah and Ten Commandments into secu-lar languages paved the way for future Jewish worship in the Diaspora. Lest one think that the Torah should be studied and practiced only in the Land of

---

[1] *Deuteronomy* 2:5. See *Midrash* Tanchuma, *Devarim* 2. There were seventy nations in Biblical days, hence the seventy languages. See footnote 6.

[2] Babylonian Talmud, *Shabbat* 88b.

[3] *Genesis* 31:47 and *Exodus* 13:16.

Israel, these foreign words would testify that Torah is not in the exclusive domain of Hebrew-speaking countries.[4]

Yet there must be more to teaching Torah in foreign languages. Because when Jews came to Babylon and established the right to practice Judaism in a non-Hebrew-speaking country, they started to teach the Torah, and write the Talmud, in Aramaic. It could be argued that Aramaic was the Jewish vernacular, and so our Sages taught and wrote in a language understood by most Jews of that time. Still, once the right to study Torah in Babylon was established, why did they persist in teaching in Aramaic? There is something to be said for teaching Torah in G-d's language — but our Sages did not even make an effort to teach it in the Holy Tongue.

LINGUISTIC ORIGINS
The seventy languages originated at the Tower of Babel. In 1764 BCE, seventy nations gathered to build a tower, from which they planned to wage war against G-d. The group was perfectly united in their heresy. As a fitting punishment, G-d divided them, causing each to speak its own language. Divided along linguistic lines, they could no longer cooperate in their joint endeavor. Instructions and requests drew blank stares or incorrect responses. The nations soon grew frustrated and dispersed.[5]

IS IT APPROPRIATE?
The Tower of Babel was not built of stone, but of brick. Bricks are man-made, but stones are created by G-d. This is precisely the difference between Hebrew and other languages. Other languages are products of human convention. But Hebrew is the Divine tongue, its letters formed by G-d.

This only underlines the question, however: why should Torah be studied in languages of human convention? [6]

---

[4] See Kedushat Levi and Ktav Sofer on *Deuteronomy* 2:5.

[5] *Genesis* 11:1–9.

[6] See Likutei Sichot VI, p. 13–25.

Furthermore, we see from this biblical account that secular languages were spawned in the heresy of the Tower of Babel. Should languages spawned in heresy be used to translate the sacred words of our Torah?

EVERYTHING MUST SERVE

Our Sages taught that all creation must serve to enhance G-d's glory. If this is true even of physical objects, it must surely be true of languages, even languages of human convention.[7]

Moreover, letters and words are vessels that contain ideas, sentiments, and knowledge. Because all knowledge stems from G-d, there must be a spark of Divinity in every letter, regardless of its language. If the languages of the world are not used in Torah study or prayer, the Divine sparks embedded in them remain forever captive in their secular mold.

When G-d uttered the Ten Commandments in all seventy languages, he bridged the gap between the Tower of Babel letters of heresy and the Hebrew letters of faith, and thus elevated the secular language for use in Divine service. Similarly, Moses' translation of Torah into all seventy languages empowered us to draw the secular and mundane into the sanctity of Torah.[8]

REMOVING THE BULWARK

Why did Moses wait nearly forty years before he translated the Torah? Why were G-d's translations of the Ten Commandments not heard by the nations? Because of Sichon and Og, monarchs of the Emorite and Bashanite kingdoms.

Neighboring nations paid these powerful and influential kingdoms to defend their borders against the Jewish armies. The Jewish mystics saw in these kingdoms not only a physical bulwark against the Jews, but also a spiritual bulwark against the Torah. These two kingdoms resisted the Torah's influence over the seventy nations, and the Torah's use of the seventy languages.

---

[7] Ethics of our Fathers 5:11.

[8] Shem MiShmuel 5676, on Deuteronomy 2:5 and Torah Ohr on *ShemotShemot* 87b.

When these powerful kingdoms were finally vanquished, the resistance they had spearheaded was finally overcome, and Moses was permitted to translate the Torah. The path was now paved for the secular to be sublimated and the mundane uplifted. The seventy languages could now be drawn into the sacred realm of Torah.[9]

This is why our Sages wrote many Torah books in secular languages rather than in the Holy Tongue. The Talmud was written in Aramaic. Maimonides wrote in Arabic. Rashi often translated Hebrew words into French. This tradition continues today, when we study the Torah in English and many other contemporary languages.

Whenever the Torah is taught in a secular language, the letters and sentences of that language are imbued with sanctity and the sparks of holiness that have been lying dormant within them are redeemed. This process gradually purifies our world and brings us ever closer to the time of total Divine revelation: the Messianic era.

This process was started by our ancestors. But it is you and I — ordinary Jews of today — who are charged with, and empowered to, complete the task. We don't have to reinvent the wheel; we simply need to expand on the efforts they made.

---

[9] *Shem MiShmuel* 5676, and *Sfat Emet* 5646, on *Deuteronomy* 2:5. This helps us understand why our triumph over these two monarchs and their countries is emphasized in King David's ode of praise to G-d (*Psalms* 136) for the Exodus from Egypt.

"So we're supposed to be living on earth for a Heavenly purpose. Does that mean that we shouldn't derive enjoyment from life's physical pleasures?"

THE SACRED BARBECUE
WHAT OF THE SOUL?

Sunshine bathes the backyard; birds chirp atop the trees as a gentle breeze rustles their leaves. Sounds of playing children and the pleasant conversation of adults mingle with the aroma of sizzling steak. This typical summer scene — the camaraderie and relaxed atmosphere of an outdoor barbecue — tantalizes our bodily senses.

But what of our soul? Is *she* enjoying this, too? Can taking in a ballgame or digging into a barbecued steak be labeled "Divine service"?

THE ANIMAL SERVES

"When G-d will broaden your boundary, and you will say, 'My soul desires to eat meat' — eat as much meat as your soul desires."[1] We are familiar with our soul's desire for prayer and good deeds. We are familiar with soulful yearnings for G-d. But who ever heard of a soulful desire for meat?

Everything that G-d created, He created for His glory.[2] This means that all things physical could and should be used to serve and to glorify the Creator. Every physical object contains a spark of Divinity. As humans, we have been granted the gift of actualizing the potential within this spark. The spark within us is relatively easy to actualize; every time we pray, study, or fulfill one of the commandments, we express our Divine spark.

The spark in an animal is not so fortunate. It is constrained within a body whose instincts limit its degree of expression. There is no cognitive thought, intelligent expression, or freedom of choice in an animal. However, when we eat of its meat, and utilize the energy gained from this to perform a noble

---

[1] Deuteronomy 12:20.

[2] Ethics of Our Fathers 6:11.

REACHING FOR G-D

deed or to engage in devout prayer, the animal's Divine spark partakes in our mitzvah and thus fulfills its purpose in the service of G-d.

So the next time we attend a barbecue, and our mouth waters at the aroma of sizzling meat, let's remember that our soul is "salivating," too. It is yearning and anticipating liberating the Divine spark that is embedded within the meat.

PERSONAL BENEFIT

Liberating that spark benefits not only the animal, but also us. Embedded within a coarse animal, the spark's insistent and unceasing yearning for freedom has built up a torrent of pent-up energy and sacred desire. As we liberate the spark, we open its floodgates, and channel its incredibly sacred energy into ourselves; thus enhancing our own desire for G-d.

But everything depends on our intention. A barbecue could be nothing more than a hedonistic indulgence — or it could be an opportunity to elevate spiritually inferior matter to a higher realm.

BLOOD EQUALS PASSION

This is why the Torah prohibits drinking the animal's blood. "Be strong and do not consume the blood. For the blood is the soul [life force]."[3]

Blood represents passion and excitement — the life force. When our passion for meat is sacred, when meat is a vehicle in our service of G-d, then our meat eating becomes a sacred act in the service of the Divine. On the other hand, when our passion lies in the meat itself (drinking the animal's blood, as it were) we forfeit the inherent sanctity involved, and transgress G-d's holy Will.

The real question is whether we choose to lower our noble purpose as humans to the level of the animal, or whether we will ride the synergy of

---

[3] Deuteronomy 12:23.

animal and human to a higher level. The former unleashes our own animalistic instincts. The latter liberates a sacred spark.[4]

This is why the Torah concludes, *"You shall not consume its [the animal's] soul along with the meat."*[5] The Divine spark contained within the animal is its very soul. If we succumb to the animal's "blood" by allowing our passions to be overwhelmed by the meat rather than by the spiritual spark within it, we consume (i.e., destroy) the animal's soul along with its body.

Such consumption is hedonistic and wasteful; it cannot be labeled Divine. We are capable of better. We are expected to bring our soul along with us to the barbecue, and discover the Divine spark within the meat. When we do that, we come away strengthened; newly fortified by a fresh Divine spark. [6]

Every bite can be enjoyable and delicious — to the body and to the soul.

---

[4] Of course, it is possible to liberate the spark retroactively through proper repentance, provided the meat is kosher. See Tanya, ch. 7.

[5] *Deuteronomy* 12:23.

[6] This essay is based in part on *Torat Moshe* (Rabbi Moshe Sofer) on *Deuteronomy* 12:20. See Torat Moshe (Rabbi Moshe Alshich, Tzfat), ibid. for an alternative explanation.

REACHING FOR G-D

Living on earth for a Heavenly purpose offers meaning and inspiration. What if we allow earthly attractions to distract us from our holy purpose? Are there any reflections that will inspire us to return?

LINKING TO THE DIVINE
TRUE GREATNESS

We live in a big world. What we know of it is incredible, and what we don't is immeasurable. Exploring the vast expanse, the unlimited potential, the endless promise —characterizes the magnificent, thrilling experience that is life. There is no end to knowledge and no end to exploration. There is no end to travel and no end to discovery. There is always a new horizon, always a grand plateau. Who could grow tire of such exploration?

As Jews, this question gives us pause. True, the universe is vast, but surely there is more to life than the mere exploration of a finite universe. The great Rabbi Shimon spent thirteen years in a cave in the Galilean hills. When he emerged, he could not countenance society's behavior. Men scurried about, working for their livelihood. Women scrubbed and washed. Children whiled away their time. "What folly!" he mused. "To reject eternity for temporal gain.[1]

Would Rabbi Shimon think highly of the grandeur described above? Voyages across oceans and deep into the sea, travel to outer space, anthropological exploration of ancient civilizations, and the unquenchable thirst for sciences are all inspiring — but Rabbi Shimon wouldn't qualify them as true grandeur. Love of family, hobbies, and careers are important, but they are not the epitome of greatness.

True greatness cannot be measured in finite terms. It is measured only by the infinite expanse of the Divine and by the extent of our relationship with Him.

---

[1] *Babylonian Talmud, Shabbat33b.*

Contemporary Mitzrayim

Our Sages taught us to regard the Exodus from Egypt as a contemporary event, one that takes place every year, in every generation. Taken literally, this teaching can be perplexing to someone who has never set foot in Egypt. But our Sages were referring to a higher plane, a different kind of Egypt, a different form of Exodus.

The Hebrew word for Egypt, *Mitzrayim*, has two meanings. It means "Egypt," but it also means "confinement." Our world is a world of confinement; our minds are the most confined of all. We cannot imagine, let alone comprehend, the G-dly realm that lies beyond us, a world that is truly beautiful, infinitely meaningful, eternally noble — yet, completely unknowable. We often act as if that realm does not exist; as if that vast expanse of brilliant splendor is irrelevant to us. We concern ourselves with the tangible and empirical, the limited sliver of knowledge accessible to the human brain; we are completely oblivious to the true beauty that lies beyond. [2]

---

[2] For example, let's consider time and space, two elements of existence. To G-d, Who is eternal, past, present, and future are one. He created time. He is present in what we call the past, just as He is present in what we call the future.

Compare this absolute freedom of time/space to our own limited existence. We exist only in the present. We occupy our space and only our space. You cannot sit in my space while I sit in it, and I cannot sit in your space while you sit in it. The same is true with time. We exist only in the present, which is in continuous flux. By the time you read this line, the present from the previous line has already passed and a new present has arrived. Try as we may, we cannot travel back to the past or forward into the future. We are confined to the infinitesimal present that moves along with us through the continuum of time.

G-d is not confined to the present or to one space. We, on the other hand, are severely confined. Yet no one seems to exhibit symptoms of claustrophobia from this confinement. Why is that? Because we are blissfully oblivious to our confinement. We assume that we are free and have no idea that a greater level of freedom could exist.

Similarly, we believe that our world is great, and we have no understanding of G-d's true greatness.

This is the confinement to which the Hebrew word *mitzrayim* alludes. This confinement was exemplified by Ancient Egypt, a nation of stunning achievement. The Egyptians made great strides in the sciences and in mathematics, but were oblivious to G-d. They were led by an idolatrous Pharaoh, who refused to acknowledge the superiority, the very existence, of G-d. This *mitzrayim* is indeed contemporary. It is not just an ancient phenomenon; we labor under it every day.

REACHING BEYOND THE CONFINEMENT

Yet we are not doomed to this confinement-of-the-mind; we can break out. This is the spiritual Exodus from Egypt. When our ancestors left Egypt, they were also granted an Exodus from their spiritual "Egypt," their confinement-of-the-mind. They learned that any quest for true greatness must lead to G-d.

How does a finite human make contact with an infinite G-d? Through the fulfillment of His commandments and the study of His Torah. When we reach into our pockets to help a person in need, we overcome our selfish nature and touch the Divine. When we devote ourselves to teaching children about life, morality, and G-d, we serve a purpose greater than ourselves.

When we pour our hearts into prayer and allow our souls to tremble in ecstasy, we sense a glimmer of infinity. When we contemplate the majesty of our Creator and intuit His Presence in our daily lives, we experience a fragment of the sublime. When we study the sacred words of Torah uttered in celestial splendor at Sinai, when we attempt to recapture through meditation the rapture of experiencing the Divine, we enter, if for but a fleeting moment, the magnificent and eternal domain.

We discern, if for but a fleeting moment, the true meaning of life. These moments are fleeting, but they are also eternal. They grace us with the potential to reach for infinity and to touch it, too.

As years turn to decades, as we enter the twilight of our life, we each face the question that all mortals need to ask: What have I done during the course of my life to reach beyond the confinement and touch on life's truest meaning?

Have I plumbed life's richest depths? Have I discovered the pulse of the Divine?[3]

If we apply ourselves today, we will be satisfied with the answers that we will have to offer tomorrow.

---

[3] This essay is based on a talk given by Rabbi Menachem M. Schneersohn, the Lubavitcher Rebbe, on January 22, 1983.

REACHING FOR G-D

"You seem so sure of my abilities. What makes you so certain that I can bring Heaven down to earth?"

A CONFIDENT FATHER

BLESSED BEGINNINGS

Many restrictions are placed on *Kohanim*, the priestly class. They are forbidden, with rare exceptions, to attend funerals, lest they become ritually impure. They are restricted in whom they may marry. This is because they have an exalted status of purity, and they are required to guard it.[1]

One would imagine that young children in the priestly families would be introduced gradually to this exalted but rigorous way of life. It would be understandable if parents would want to shield their children from these demands in their delicate early years. Yet the Torah permits no such thing.

The Torah introduces the *Kohen's* strictures with the words, "Talk to the Kohanim, sons of Aaron, and talk to them." Biblical commentators understood the repetition of the words "talk to them," as a commandment to educate the youth.[2] In other words, talk to the elders so that they may talk to (educate) their children.

HIGH EXPECTATIONS

With this instruction, the Torah not only obligates the parents, but also proclaims that this can indeed be expected from the youth. To expect children to understand the fine nuances of higher devotion, and to accept the burdens that make this devotion possible, may seem very demanding to us, but the Torah assures us that it is well within their capability.[3]

---

[1] Leviticus 21:1-9.

[2] *Babylonian Talmud, Yevamot* 114a. See also Rashi's commentary to *Leviticus* 21:19.

[3] The Torah uses the Hebrew word *"emor,"* which means talk, rather than the more conventional *"daber,"* which means speak. In Hebrew, *daber* has a connotation of firm presentation; *emor* connotes soft persuasion. In using the softer term, the Torah instructs the adults to guide the children gently through the complex labyrinth of the priestly strictures. It instructs them to persuade and to inspire

In Every Jew

Though this instruction is directed to the youth of the priestly families, it is also incorporated into the Torah, which was given to the entire nation. This indicates that the teaching inherent in this instruction and the assurance regarding our capability are also directed to the entire nation.

There are adults who are mature in age but are still children in matters of Torah. Such people might be skilled and sophisticated in other areas, but they are underdeveloped in religious instruction. They might not have been exposed to Torah in their youth and never learned to embrace its way of life. Or they might have been raised with Torah, but still find themselves with far to grow. In a sense, we are all children and we are all addressed in this verse. By obligating all Jews to be personally active in the religious education of these "children," G-d proclaims that it is indeed within the ability of every Jew to absorb Torah teachings and to be inspired by them.

But what gave the priestly youth, and by extension every Jewish child, the potential for such exalted devotion and inspiration? The answer lies in the matzah that our ancestors ate when they left Egypt.

In Haste

During and after their Exodus from Egypt, our ancestors ate unleavened bread.[4] The Torah tells us that they tried to bake bread, but that because they left in haste, they did not have time to let the dough rise. This curious statement seems to belie the facts. Our ancestors had ample time to bake their bread before they left Egypt.[5] Furthermore, they could have carried their

---

the children — to help them see this sacred path as a wonderful privilege rather than as a difficult burden. This command is evidence of the young *Kohanim*'s ability to rise to this task.

[4] *Exodus* 12:39. The Exodus took place on the fifteenth of Nissan, and the manna began to fall on the fifteenth of Iyar. The matzah lasted for thirty days.

[5] Moses informed them of the Exodus at least five (if not fifteen) full days before they actually left (see *Exodus* 12:1–15). In fact, they did prepare matzah to eat be-

dough with them as they left Egypt, and baked their bread when they first camped. That would have provided ample time for the dough to rise.

HUMBLE BREAD

It is human nature to feel small and insignificant when we encounter true greatness. When we meet someone of great stature, we feel overwhelmed. On the night of their Exodus, as they were kneading their dough, G-d descended from Heaven to free them from slavery. At this most exalted level of Divine revelation, our ancestors naturally responded with supreme humility.

However, this experience was not limited to our ancestors. It was experienced by the whole of creation.[6] The dough did not rise — because nothing rises in the Presence of G-d. Just as the ego remains humble in G-d's Presence, so did the dough.[7] It was not lack of time that prevented it from rising, but the Presence of its Creator. This is why we declare, on the night of Passover, that the dough did not manage to rise, before the King of kings, blessed be He, revealed Himself and freed them.[8]

That matzah, affected by G-d himself, surely left a profound impression on those who ate it. Our ancestors, who ate sixty-one meals of that matzah, from the fifteenth of Nissan to the fifteenth of Iyar, were left awed and humbled.[9] They were suffused with a continuous awareness of the Divine Omnipres-

---

fore that night, which they ate on the eve of their redemption (*Exodus* 12:8). Why could they not also have prepared dough, at that time, for their journey?

[6] Likutei Torah, *Vayikra* 12b. See also the Chassidic discourse on matzah zu in Siddur Tefillot Mikol Hashanah.

[7] Although this represents a radical transformation of the dough's nature, it is not the only incident of such transformation. When G-d split the Sea of Reeds, the waters stood upright. When G-d gave the Torah, all birds and animals were silent for the duration. It is similarly prophesied that, in the Messianic age, the "lion shall lie down with the lamb." These transformations are affected by the sudden revelation of G-d's Presence. When the Creator appears, all of creation takes note.

[8] *Haggadah* of Pesach.

[9] *Exodus* 16:1. See *Mechilta* and Rashi's commentary on this verse.

ence. They were inspired with passion and devotion; imbued with a capacity for the sacred nuances of Torah.[10]

Indeed, it works for us too. The matzah we eat on Passover empowers us to climb the ladder of spirituality.[11]

Regardless of where we are in our spiritual journey G-d proclaims our ability to succeed.

---

[10] It is noteworthy that the Torah's commandment to educate the youth, and its message of their competence to rise to this task, is chanted, in most years, close to the fifteenth of Iyar, the day our ancestors ate the last of their matzah and reached the zenith of their spiritual experience.

[11] This essay is based on a talk given by Rabbi Menachem M Schneerson, the Lubavitcher Rebbe on 15 Iyar 5745.

"You say that even when we feel inundated by the corporeal and mundane, our souls remain spiritual and pristine. You say that, within, we continue to love G-d and to yearn for Him. But what should we do when we can't hear the messages of our soul?"

THE DUEL AND DUALITY OF LIFE
BODY AND SOUL

Life, according to Torah, is a duel between two forces: the body's gravitation towards self gratification and the soul's attraction towards fulfillment and meaning. This body/soul dynamic is the crux of the human experience. Every human endeavor is influenced by this conflict. The body desires the physical benefit we draw from it, while the soul desires the value of this endeavor to the service of G-d.[1]

Pursuit of nourishment is a perfect example. This desire is experienced by both body and soul. The body craves nourishment simply because nourishment satisfies physical hunger. The soul craves nourishment because nourishment provides energy that can, in turn, be used for the purpose of Divine worship. [2]

To the body, nourishment is an end in itself. The body therefore enslaves itself to the pursuit of nourishment, devoting much time and energy to this. To the soul, nourishment is but a means to a higher end. The soul is devoted to the service of an Authority greater than itself and co-opts every experience, including the pursuit of nourishment, to this higher end. Put simply, the soul masters the eating experience and directs it to a higher purpose. The body is mastered by the eating experience and adopts it as its own purpose.[3]

Even as the body is mastered by the experience, the soul doesn't surrender. It continues to yearn for G-d and constantly works to exert and express this

---

[1] Tanya, ch. 8.

[2] Tanya, ch. 7.

[3] Tanya, ch. 23–24. See also two previous essays, "Do Jews Dig Wells?" and "The Sacred Barbecue."

yearning. Even those who regularly submit to the material domination of the body have a vibrant, living soul within. The soul continues to love G-d and worship Him at all times, even though it is forced to remain silent. This silent love is the experience of *tzaraat*.

TZARAAT – THE EXTERNAL EXPERIENCE

The Torah speaks of a condition that manifests itself through white dead patches that appear on the surface of the skin.[4] The *metzora* is often treated derisively by Scripture and classical Jewish works. The Talmud explains that *tzaraat* was a punishment for sin.[5] Yet a careful analysis yields a deeper understanding.

Let's consider the nature of the *tzaraat* affliction. It is a relatively minor disease that affects only the skin surface. The *metzora's* vital inner organs, such as the heart, brain, and liver are in good health.[6] But the vibrancy of the inner organs, while sufficient to ensure the life force within, is unable to reach the outer surface — which results in the white, dead blotches of skin. On a spir-

---

[4] *Leviticus*, ch. 15.

[5] Seven sins are specified. They are slander, murder, perjury, debauchery, pride, theft, and jealousy. Slander is the primary sin of them all. In fact, the Hebrew word *"metzora"* is an amalgam of two words: *"motzi ra"* (publicizing negative [information]). For more detail, see *Babylonian Talmud, Arachin* 16a. See also *Zohar, Leviticus*, p. 53a.

[6] *Likutei Torah, Leviticus* p. 22b. See also *Sefer Hitvaaduot,* 5751, p. 155. The Torah indicates that the *tzaraat* afflicts only the skin. Not the flesh, nor the bone, and certainly *not the* inner organs. Though some English Bibles translate *tzaraat* as leprosy, the afflictions should not be confused. Leprosy is a medical condition brought about by natural phenomena, bacteria which affect the nervous system, muscles, and circulation. This condition is correctly treated by medical doctors. The *tzaraat* affliction was a miraculous phenomenon brought about by Divine intervention, as a response to a person's moral condition. It was treated by the priest. A physician can address physical symptoms only, not spiritual causes. The priest, as a conduit of G-d's blessing, could help one reconnect to G-d, thus eliminating the cause and relieving the symptom. *Yad Hachazakah, Hilchot Tumat Tzaraat* 17:10.

itual level this is symbolic of those with fully functioning souls, who are inwardly, perhaps even subconsciously, consumed by love for G-d, but whose passion doesn't translate externally by influencing their behavior.[7]

DISENGAGEMENT

How can this condition be resolved? The Torah instructs that the *metzora* be quarantined for seven days. If interaction with the secular and mundane arouses material cravings that drown out the cry of the soul, then we must temporarily disengage from them, divest ourselves from exposure to the secular element, and focus on the constant, though silenced, cry of our soul.

This quarantine must last for seven days — one full week. A full cycle of introspection and spiritual pursuit must pass, during which time the soul is given full expression and the body is retrained to harness the mundane to the service of G-d.[8]

REENGAGEMENT

This sheltered period is, at once, blissful and anathema to the soul. Blissful because the soul is permitted to pursue its cause unhampered, and anathema because the soul's ultimate objective is to sanctify the mundane through utilizing it for the worship of G-d.

This is why, when the seven days are over, it is incumbent on the *metzora* to emerge from quarantine. He must come forward and be inspected by the priest to determine if the condition has passed. If the white skin patches are still visible, the *metzora* returns to quarantine, because the spiritual vitality within has not yet reached the outer surface. If the priest determines that the disease has passed, the *metzora* reenters society and the world at large. He must reengage, but this time with more regard for the soul's interest than for that of the body.

---

[7] Sfat Emet 5647, Metzora.

[8] Sefer Hachinuch, Mitzvah 169. See also Sfat Emet 5647, Metzora.

The same holds true for us. Material distractions numb our hearts to the yearning of our souls. When this happens we must identify those activities that embolden our materialistic urges and disengage from them. However, with time we must learn to reengage those areas of life in ways that are spiritually healthy. Because is not our objective to disengage from life. Our objective is to achieve harmony between body and soul.

AVOIDING *TZARAAT*

We now know how to heal from the *tzaraat* affliction. But what helps a Jew to avoid it in the first place?

Torah study.

In describing the healing process from *tzaraat*, the Biblical text mentions the word "Torah" five times, which our commentators say is an allusion to the Five Books of Moses. Study of Torah is the greatest shield against the spiritual disconnection that causes *tzaraat*.[9] The Torah binds its student, the Jew, to its Author — G-d. And in a way that precludes spiritual disconnection.[10]

When the message of our soul is drowned out by the voices of the mundane, all we need to do is pay better attention. Fortified by our bond with G-d, our souls are empowered to win this duel.

---

[9] *Vayikra Rabbah* 16:6.
[10] Tanya, ch. 13.

"Our goals are so lofty; our intentions are the best. But aren't these lofty goals and wonderful intentions worthless — if we see that we don't live up to them?"

ABRAHAM'S PLEA
CRUEL AND UNUSUAL

Societies vary in their values and beliefs. Yet there are some fundamental convictions that are at the core of all civilized societies. The value of life is one of these. Whether or not we can provide a rational explanation for why murder is wrong, our very souls are repulsed by the deliberate or negligent taking of life. When an individual or culture demonstrates disregard for this value, we consider this criminal or evil. We cringe at the annihilation of innocent people and find the notion of collective punishment unconscionable.

The populations of Sodom and Gomorrah were so corrupt that G-d decided to destroy them.[1] We identify with the necessity of punishing those who are guilty, but it is difficult to imagine that every person in the city was deserving of death. We suppose that there were at least several innocents in the city, and we cringe at the thought that, through no fault of their own, they were to be slaughtered alongside the wicked. A sense of injustice is aroused within us, and we identify with Abraham's cry, "Far be it from You to do a thing such as this! To put to death the righteous with the wicked!"

At the same time, we would tremble to speak this way before G-d. We marvel at Abraham's audacity as he spoke these words, and are surprised at his tone. After all, he was talking to G-d! Given his faith and conviction, how could he brazenly challenge G-d?

MAN OF FAITH

Abraham was a man of perfect faith; he followed G-d's every command with unerring loyalty. If G-d commanded it, Abraham knew it was just. He sent away his concubine and their son, circumcised himself in his old age, and was prepared to sacrifice his only son — all at G-d's command. Abraham

---

[1] *Genesis* 18:25.

trusted implicitly that anything G-d wants must be good. Yet when G-d informed Abraham that Sodom and Gomorrah would be destroyed, he was appalled. Notwithstanding his perfect faith, he demanded reconsideration, "Would you slay the righteous alongside the wicked? Will not the Judge of all the earth do justice?" Here stands Abraham, a man of unwavering faith, accusing G-d of injustice and possibly even murder![2]

LIGHT AND DARKNESS

On the first day of Creation, G-d separated light from darkness.[3] The Midrash explains that the words "light" and "darkness" refer not only to physical light and darkness, but are also metaphors for the righteous and the wicked. Thus, the verse would read, "On the first day, G-d separated the righteous from the wicked."[4] What was the purpose of separating the righteous from the wicked?

The Chassidic masters clarify and expound on this. Individuals are judged on their own merit; they are rewarded for their good deeds and punished for their sins. In addition to individual trials, G-d also tries the human race as a whole. If the whole human race would fall into depravity, the world would be destroyed. When only a minority of humanity is depraved, the world is preserved on account of the righteous majority.

The verdict from following the majority rule would indeed mean that if the majority were righteous, the wicked minority would be absorbed into the status of the righteous majority, and thus the world would be spared. How-

---

[2] That Abraham spoke so harshly, despite his otherwise gentle and generous nature, underscores his vast love for humanity. When people were endangered, Abraham was not ambivalent, and could not allow himself to be gentle. This should serve as a lesson to us all, not only for those times when our fellow is threatened with physical danger, but also for those times when our fellow faces spiritual danger, such as assimilation and the like. (Likutei Sichot, vol. XI, pp. 58–59)

[3] *Genesis* 1:4.

[4] *Bereishit Rabbah* 2:5 and 18:25.

ever, applying this rule in the opposite situation would pose a problem. If the wicked were in the majority, the law of majority rule would dictate that the world be destroyed, and the entire human race, including the righteous, would perish. A law originally designed as an instrument of compassion would serve as an instrument of cruelty.

To prevent this unthinkable consequence, G-d introduced a new rule (an exception to the usual method of judgment) that would override the standard jurisprudence of majority rule. If the wicked ever ascend to the majority, G-d would "separate" the righteous from the wicked, allowing the minority of the righteous to be judged on their own merit; humanity would thus survive through the righteous who would be spared. On the very first day of Creation, G-d introduced this exception to the majority rule, to ensure the survival of humanity. [5]

BACK TO ABRAHAM

This insight lends new perspective to Abraham's words. When Abraham heard that the entire population of the Sodom region would die, he assumed that G-d would apply the established jurisprudence of majority rule. For it was only when judging all of humanity that G-d had "separated the righteous" to judge them on their own merit and thus save the human race. Since this was not a judgment of humanity, but only of Sodom, and the human race was not in peril, Abraham assumed that G-d would permit the rule of the majority to stand. Any remaining righteous individuals would be punished along with the wicked.

He pleaded with G-d to view the judgment of Sodom in global terms. He reminded G-d that out of concern for humanity, "the Judge of the entire earth" chose to suspend the rule of the majority by separating the righteous from the wicked. If so, pleaded Abraham, might not an entire city be granted similar compassion in its judgment? Viewed in this light, Abraham's words are offered not in insolent protest, but as a wise legal appeal. "Shall not the Judge of the entire earth do justice?" Is it not true that when You judge the

---

[5] See Panim Yafot on Genesis 1:4.

entire earth, you waive the majority rule and do justice separately to the righteous? Will You not provide the same justice to Sodom that you do to the entire earth?[6]

How did G-d respond? G-d actually appreciated Abraham's argument, and assured him that the righteous people of Sodom would not be slain. In fact, G-d asserted, "Had I discovered even ten righteous ones in all Sodom, I would have spared the entire city."[7] But unfortunately, there were no righteous people in Sodom.[8]

PERSONAL APPLICATION

The dialogue between Abraham and G-d teaches us an important lesson. We often judge ourselves within the courtroom of our own strict opinion. We are all too familiar with our weaknesses, and we allow them to govern our self-perception.

The human psyche is naturally filled with glitches. We are jealous, insecure, arrogant, narcissistic. We are indulgent, greedy, dishonest, impatient. The list continues. When we look closely, it becomes difficult to remain upbeat. We think, "If I am so faulty, limited, and weak, I must be a failure." But when the precision of an honest measuring stick creates despondency, the force of Abraham's plea challenges us with astounding relevance.

---

[6] In kabbalistic terms, Abraham pleaded with G-d to arise from His Throne of Strict Justice and sit on His Throne of Compassion. Rabbeinu Bachya explains that this is why Abraham continually addressed G-d here as Elokim (Judge), and G-d consistently responded with His Four-Letter Name of Compassion. Abraham thought that G-d was sitting in stern judgment of Sodom, but in truth G-d was already seated on the Throne of Compassion. See also Nachmanides on *Genesis* 18:20.

[7] *Genesis* 18:32.

[8] See Rabbeinu Bachya, who explains that the power of ten to save the entire city underscores the importance and sanctity of a *minyan* (minimum quorum of ten men for purposes of congregational prayer). For more information, see Igeret Hakodesh, ch. 23.

When the entire earth is judged, the righteous are not punished on account of the wicked; they are judged on their own merit. Similarly, when we make a comprehensive self-evaluation we ought not to dismiss our redeeming factors just because they are scarce. In fact, just as we would be horrified to learn that good people have been condemned along with the bad, so should we be averse to dismissing our strengths and labeling ourselves failures.

Just as we must be aware of our weaknesses, so must we be aware of our strengths. They are our redeeming factors and they will lead us back on the road toward success. If the righteous were slain on account of the wicked, humanity would become extinct. Likewise, if we dismiss our strengths, because of our weaknesses, we assure our own failure and slowly extinguish our spirit. After the Great Flood, one righteous family rebuilt the entire human race.[9] Similarly, highlighting our strengths, even if they are few, will allow our redeeming qualities to thrive and will help us redeem ourselves.

Despite our countless, repetitive, and serious failings, we mustn't be too hard on ourselves. Instead, we must seek out our strengths and build on them.

---

[9] The rule of the majority was suspended during the Great Flood. Noah and his family lived alongside the wicked, who were slated for punishment. Yet G-d spared the righteous, and thus ensured the survival of humanity and other species. Furthermore, immediately following the Flood, G-d made a covenant never to bring such total destruction against humanity again. Though the covenant referred only to total destruction by Flood, Abraham saw it as referring to all forms of punishment. In this context, Abraham's words can be interpreted as a statement rather than a question: "The Judge of all the earth shall not do justice [but shall do mercy]." The One Who judged the entire earth during the Flood has made a covenant never to mete out such (blanket) justice again. (See *Bereishit Rabbah* 49:9 and Ohr HaChayim on *Genesis* 9:11.)

"This is all very fine for those who were raised in a traditional home, and are accustomed to doing the many *mitzvot*. But what of those of us who weren't, and aren't?"

FREEDOM TO SERVE
PRIORITIES

I recently asked a young man if he would like to take upon himself the fulfillment of a certain mitzvah. His reply caught me by surprise. "It's not my cup of tea," he told me. It made me wonder if we Jews are limited to a predetermined direction, or if we are really capable of more. On the chessboard of life, are we pawns, who can travel in only one direction? Or are we queens, who can strike out in the direction of our choice?

THE ANGEL

Angels are unidirectional. Their characters are created by G-d as single, predetermined profiles. They must remain on those predetermined tracks and are incapable of lateral movement.[1] Some angels serve G-d in love. Others serve G-d with joy. Angels who love are incapable of joy, and angels with joy are incapable of love, unless they "borrow" from each other. A loving angel who wants to worship with joy must borrow joy from a joyful angel. A joyful angel who wishes to pray with love must borrow love from a loving angel. The same holds true for every angelic characteristic.

This is why the prophet describes angels as stationary. The angel cannot abandon its post and take up a new position, unless it is commanded to do so. It is capable of tremendous devotion and spiritual passion, but it is inca-

---

[1] This is why angels pray in groups. (*Isaiah* 6:3) They call out to each other and seek each other's permission to break out of their predetermined characteristics. Why must they seek such permission? Because angels are confined to their predetermined characteristics and cannot escape them, unless assisted by other angels. See Likutei Torah, p. 1a.

REACHING FOR G-D

pable of moving away from itself. Or of doing things in ways that are different from the nature imparted to it by G-d.[2]

THE JEW

Are we different? Are we confined to those *mitzvot* that we deem "priority"? King Solomon refers to the Jewish People as G-d's bride. If G-d is the King, then we are His queen. This means that, on the chessboard of life, the Jewish soul is capable of multidirectional travel, like that of the queen.[3]

We are each unique. We each have our own characteristics and prefer our own path of worship. Some of us are meditative, others active. Some are joyful, others loving. Some like to study, others to do kind deeds. Our paths are unique to ourselves. But here is where we differ from angels. Angels cannot veer from their characters; we can.

The prophet describes the soul as mobile. It is capable of lateral movement. Though we each have a favorite beginning place, a mitzvah that our nature most prefers, we are also able to act in ways that are not inherent to our character. We are capable of performing those *mitzvot* that are not our "priority."[4] We are capable of all *mitzvot*, despite our preference for one of them. We can choose any path of serving G-d, even those paths we were not raised in, even those paths that are not indigenous to our comfort zones.

CAN WE THRIVE?

The astute reader will ask, "Souls may be able to perform outside of their comfort zones, but can they thrive? Should we not perform with alacrity those *mitzvot* that we do enjoy, rather than perform with reluctance those *mitzvot* that we don't enjoy?"

---

[2] *Zachariah* 3:7. See commentary Torah Ohr, p. 30a.

[3] Shir Hashirim 3:11, 5:1.

[4] See note 2 above. Talmudic rabbis would adopt and cherish one mitzvah above all others. They observed all the mitzvot, but they singled out one mitzvah for preference. *Babylonian Talmud, Shabbat* 118b.

To answer this question, let us consider the twelve sons of Jacob, the roots of our nation. These twelve men were the fathers of our people; each imprinted his offspring with the unique strains of his character.

JACOB'S BLESSING

Just before his passing, Jacob blessed his sons. Each son received a blessing consistent with his path of spiritual service. Judah was blessed with leadership, Issachar with diligent scholarship, Zebulun with business acumen, etc.

After Jacob blessed each son individually, he repeated all the blessings to each of his sons.[5] Why did he do that? What benefit could each derive from blessings that were not conducive to developing his own strengths and achieving his own aspirations?

Jacob wanted his children to enjoy all forms of spiritual service, not only those consistent with their individual characters. He wanted them to engage in all *mitzvot*, not only those within their natural comfort zones. Jacob therefore offered individual blessings first, to inspire them towards those *mitzvot* that were consistent with their personalities. Then he conferred on them comprehensive blessings, to engender a genuine enthusiasm for all *mitzvot*, even those inconsistent with their personalities.

WE CAN THRIVE

The answer to our earlier question is: yes, we can thrive outside of our comfort zone. The differences in our spiritual constitution are derived from the unique characters of Jacob's twelve sons. But Jacob's general blessing, which enabled his sons to transcend their limitations and enjoy all manner of spiritual service, endows us too with that wonderful ability.

All Jews, regardless of background or level of observance, are equal heirs to Jacob's blessing. No mitzvah is beyond our potential. Every mitzvah can be our "cup of tea." A tradesman is, due to Jacob's blessing, able to study Torah with total devotion and concentration. A Torah scholar is, when necessary,

---

[5] *Exodus* 28: 28. See Rashi's commentary ibid.

able to leave his studies and raise funds for charitable causes, with total sincerity and joy. Every mitzvah is available to every Jew — not only to fulfill, but also to enjoy.

The next time someone tells you, "It's not my cup of tea," go out and brew another cup. Urge him or her to try it, and say that it's a new flavor. Say that it's the flavor of our forefather Jacob.[6]

Regardless of where we are raised, every mitzvah is ingrained within the very fabric of every Jewish soul. Its practice might be new to us, but its essence has been a part of us since the days of our Father Jacob.

---

[6] This essay is based on a talk given by Rabbi Menachem M. Schneersohn, the Lubavitcher Rebbe, on 15 Tevet 5744. Sefer Hisvaaduyos, pp. 743–748 and Likutei Sichot, vol. XXV, pp. 285–292.

"Growth is possible. Growth is expected. But sometimes the task seems overwhelming! How can this not make us anxious? How can I not be paralyzed with anxiety?"

THE CONFIDENT APPROACH
COLD FEET
Many years ago, I found myself in a plane, high above the Grand Canyon. I was on my way to a job as head counselor of a West Coast summer day camp. Suddenly, I began to doubt myself. Was this job right for me? Was I good enough? What had I gotten myself into? A swarm of butterflies seemed to flutter in the pit of my stomach.

This experience was new to me then. But today, many years later, it's a familiar companion. I experience it every time I take up a new challenge in life. I felt it on the day before my wedding, the day I became a father, before I accepted my first pulpit position, and before my first public lecture.

Today, the butterflies and I are no longer strangers. I welcome them heartily. They still shake my confidence, but after the initial shock I learn to ignore them and focus on the task at hand. I view the apprehension they bring as assurance that the endeavor on which I am about to embark is worthwhile.

SLACKENING AND APATHY
The Torah tells us that our ancestors journeyed from a place called *Refidim* to the Sinai Desert. Clarifying why the Torah found it necessary to spell out that *Refidim* was the place from which they set out, our Sages explain that they arrived at Sinai in a *"Refidim"* state of mind.[1]

The etymological root of the name *Refidim* is the Hebrew word *rifyon*, which means slackening. Our ancestors experienced a slackening of enthusiasm, a sense of anxiety, as they approached their encounter at Sinai.[2] G-d had singled them out from among the nations to bestow His mandate upon them.

---

[1] *Exodus* 19:2.
[2] *Mechilta* on Exodus 17:8.

Well aware of what it meant to be chosen by G-d, they worried that they were unworthy. They had lived for more than two centuries in the midst of Egyptian idolatry and depravity. Could they repent, and totally transform themselves, in the seven short weeks before they would arrive at Sinai? Could they live a righteous and exalted life? Were they worthy of the task?[3]

During their sojourn in *Refidim*, our ancestors were attacked by the tribe of *Amalek*.[4] The *Midrash* relates that when our ancestors left Egypt, the nations of the world trembled before them and were afraid to engage them in war. *Amalek* was the only tribe with the temerity to attack them.[5] Though *Amalek* was roundly defeated, his brazen act destroyed the aura of invincibility that surrounded our ancestors.

The kabbalists taught that *Amalek* represents the characteristic of coldness and apathy. He disparages our awe for the Torah, mocks our passion for G-d, scoffs at our spirituality and questions our religious convictions.[6] *Amalek's* physical attack against our ancestors paralleled his assault on their spirit. When they questioned their self-worth, they exposed themselves to *Amalek's* attack. By doubting their own ability, they made themselves vulnerable to his mockery.

Seeds of doubt are healthy; they keep our ego in check. But these seeds must never be permitted to control our state of mind. Where would I have been if I had heeded my butterflies, on that plane high above the Grand Canyon? We must focus on our abilities and strengths. Only then can we put our concerns in perspective.[7]

---

[3] This interpretation follows the Shem MiShmuel referenced in footnote 11.

[4] *Exodus* 17:8.

[5] Tanchuma, ch. 9, on *Deuteronomy* 25:18.

[6] Sefer Hamaamarim, 5680, p. 1.

[7] The *Talmud* (*Sanhedrin* 38a) teaches that Adam and Eve were created on Friday so that they would immediately enter the *Shabbat*. *Shabbat* has an uplifting effect, and G-d wanted their first experience to be uplifting. After they would be uplift-

POSITIVE THOUGHT

"I have a mean streak," a woman once complained to Rabbi Menachem M. Schneersohn, the Lubavitcher Rebbe. "I don't know why, but I refuse every favor that's asked of me. I've been in therapy for years, but it seems that I am beyond repair." The Rebbe told her that she was too focused on her faults. When a person zeroes in on his or her shortcomings, it obscures their potential for good.

The Rebbe suggested that, rather than struggle against the darkness of her soul, she should work to kindle its flame. "Don't worry about your inner conflicts just yet," the Rebbe advised. "Seek out opportunities to perform favors, and force yourself to perform them.[8]

When our ancestors arrived at Sinai, they left Refidim, the weakness of doubts, behind. They focused on their positive traits, and their confidence was bolstered. We too must learn to leave our Refidim, our weak points, behind. We too must learn to focus on the positive. We too must learn to light a candle rather than fight our own darkness. Whether it's seeking new employment opportunities, exploring possible career changes, looking for a *shidduch*, or raising children, we often fail before we succeed. It's easy to be overwhelmed by doubts of inadequacy; it's easy to despair. But it is incumbent on us to marshal our strengths and focus on the positive.

This is even truer on the spiritual front. As we consider the many commandments in the Torah, it is possible to despair of fulfilling them all. We may not have been raised with religious observance and may not be accustomed to the Torah path — though those raised in observant homes are often assailed by doubts, as well. Is it appropriate to approach G-d, when we are saddled with the sins of our past?

---

ed, they would be far better equipped to deal with their iniquities and repent for their sins.

[8] Rabbi Manis Friedman, *Doesn't Anyone Blush Anymore*, HarperCollins, 1990, p. 32.

If we focus on our negative past, on our inner *Refidim*, we will lose confidence in ourselves and slowly grow cold and apathetic toward Torah. We will become vulnerable to our inner *Amalek*, and lose our fiery passion for Judaism. The alternative is to channel our minds and thoughts toward the infinite potential of our *neshamah*, our Jewish soul.[9]

THE SOUL

Within every Jew there is a soul, a veritable portion of the Divine. The soul pines for G-d and yearns to fulfill His commandments. To the soul, every mitzvah pulses with G-dly energy, every mitzvah is a precious channel of joy and a source of pure ecstasy. We are capable of harnessing our soul's passion. We are capable of living up to G-d's mandate. But only if we try. Little by little, we can grow every day. Step by step, we can lift ourselves up.[10] [11] [12]

The path to success is strewn with doubts and fears — but paved with determination, prayer, and trust in G-d.

---

[9] This woman clearly had *reason* to be in therapy. But, as King Solomon wrote, there is a time for everything (*Ecclesiastes* 3:1). Her emotional issues obscured her ability to do good, and that barrier had to be avoided. First, she would need to be convinced that she was greater than her problems, and could act correctly despite them. Then she would be able to attack those problems. Meanwhile, her problems were attacking her. When she could prove to herself that she was capable of goodness, then she would be ready for therapy.

[10] G-d does not demand more from us than we are capable of delivering. If He issues a commandment, He endows us with the strength to follow it through. (*Babylonian Talmud, Avodah Zarah* 3a and *Bamidbar Rabbah* 12:3)

[11] This does not imply that we need not repent for our previous sins. On the contrary, repentance is one of the fundamental commandments. However, repentance is most effective when we know that we are capable of living up to G-d's expectations. Otherwise excessive dwelling on the negative can cause a loss of enthusiasm for Torah. See Tanya, chapter 27.

[12] This essay is based on Shem MiShmuel 5673.

"I'm finding constant growth to be a difficult task. My soul years, my soul is driven. I really want to soar! But my heart and mind are hard-pressed to keep pace with all those lofty aspirations ... "

THE INSIDE-OUTSIDE HOUSE

RARIFIED AIR

Shortly after the *tzaddik* Reb Mendel of Horodok arrived in Israel, a man climbed the Mount of Olives and sounded a shofar. A rumor quickly spread that the shofar's call heralded the arrival of Moshiach. When word of this reached Reb Mendel, he flung open the windows and sniffed the air, to determine if the revealed manifestation of the Divine was present — for this will be the case in the Messianic era. He then sadly closed the windows, and remarked, "Moshiach is not here. His scent is not in the air."[1]

In retelling this story, Chassidim have often asked why Reb Mendel opened the window to sniff the air outside. They concluded that Reb Mendel sniffed the air outside because, in his room, the Divine was already present.

ORDER REVERSED

This story sheds light on a *Midrashic* tale. Moses summoned his chief architect, *Betzalel,* and relayed G-d's instructions for building the Tabernacle. First he mentioned the measurements of the sacred vessels that would inhabit the Tabernacle, and then the dimensions of the Tabernacle itself.

Betzalel, the model architect, objected to the order. "As a rule," he argued, "one first builds a residence, and then its furniture."

---

[1]The term "scent" was used metaphorically, to connote an indiscernible Presence. It is worth noting the Talmudic text from *Sanhedrin* 93b: "Bar Koziba [Kochba] reigned two and a half years, and then said to the rabbis, 'I am the Moshiach.' They answered, 'Of Moshiach it is written that he smells and judges [Isaiah 11:3]. Let us see whether he [Bar Koziba] can do so.' When they saw that he was unable to judge by scent, they slew him."

Moses conceded, and exclaimed, "Indeed! Those were my precise c instructions. You must have been standing in the wings of G-d's shadow as He instructed them. You grasped His intentions perfectly."[2]

The Torah hints at this story in the verse, "*Betzalel* fulfilled all the instructions that G-d issued to Moses." Not only did *Betzalel* fulfill the instructions that Moses conveyed to him, he also intuited those instructions that G-d issued to Moses, but that Moses did not convey to him.[3]

But this narrative raises a question: Does it take a master architect to know that buildings are constructed before their furniture? The words of the story obviously contain a deeper meaning.

G-D AND PEOPLE

The purpose of the Tabernacle, and the Temple that was built after it, was to establish a domain for G-d within the physical space of our world.[4] When G-d descended upon Mount Sinai, His Presence was overwhelming; the people could not withstand the sheer intensity of the experience of direct revelation. They were physically thrown back from the mountain, and their souls expired from the spiritual intensity. G-d revived them, and dispatched angels to lead them back.[5]

After the Sinai experience, it was clear that the people could not be exposed to a direct revelation of G-d's Presence. He commanded them to build a special Tabernacle instead, where His unrestricted Presence would be manifest. Only those who were worthy and able, such as the High Priest, would access this sacred place, but its aura would affect all those outside, as well.

---

[2] The name *Betzalel* is etymologically composed of two Hebrew words, *B'tzel E-l*, which mean in the shadow of G-d. *Babylonian Talmud, Berachot* 55a.

[3] See Rashi on *Exodus* 38:22.

[4] See *Exodus* 25: 8.

[5] Exodus 28:8; *Mechilta* Exodus 20:15. *Babylonian Talmud, Shabbat* 87b.

GRADUAL TRANSFORMATION

The environment outside the chamber was not yet capable of supporting a direct revelation of Divinity. However, with effort and commitment, revelation could, over time, be made possible. According to our prophets, this will be accomplished in the Messianic era, when there will be a direct revelation of G-dliness throughout the world.[6]

The work that makes this possible is diligent study of Torah and the practice of its commandments.[7] Every time Torah is studied, a mini-revelation, like that of Mount Sinai though on a smaller scale, is effected.[8] Every object utilized in the performance of a mitzvah is enveloped by a surge of Divinity, similar to that of the Tabernacle.[9] This regular diet of Divinity gradually purifies our worldly environment and lifts the universal veil. Though it is indiscernible to us, the Jewish soul has, through millennia of effort, continually been strengthened. We are closing in on the utopia of direct revelation that will be manifest in the Messianic era.

When G-d commanded that the Tabernacle be built, He anticipated this utopia, this day when the Divinity within that sacred place would expand to envelop the entire nation, and when the human eye would see G-d and not be overwhelmed by the experience.[10]

VISION AND REALITY

Moses, a G-dly man, envisioned this utopia as well. Gazing out upon his "outside" world, he ignored its imperfections and saw only its Divine potential. His mandate was to expose the "outside" gradually to the Divine Presence on the "inside," but he yearned to accelerate the process. By building the Holy Ark before the walls that would enclose it, he hoped to offer to

---

[6] *ShemotShemot* Rabbah 29:4. Zohar, section II, p. 85. Babylonian Talmud, *Shabbat* 87b.

[7] *Isaiah* 30:20.

[8] Tanya, ch. 37.

[9] *Torah Ohr* p. 67a.

[10] Tanya, ch. 22; *Isaiah* 12:8; *Isaiah* 40:5.

the "outside" a glimpse of its own capacity and thereby activate its potential.[11]

Betzalel, the architect, was a realist. He had the patience of a man accustomed to planning for the long term. The environment on the "outside" was not prepared to host the Divine Presence just yet. He recognized that it was not appropriate to expose the Holy Ark to a yet unconditioned "outside." It would require centuries of gentle coaxing, committed coaching, and tireless training.

Moses was the visionary, *Betzalel,* the realist. Moses' vision inspired confidence in the project; *Betzalel's* realism made it materialize.

Growth is important, but it must be paced; growing too quickly can throw us off stride.

---

[11] Moses was not being unrealistic. In his presence, all *were* uplifted. Under his guidance, this was indeed possible. But Moses would not live forever. G-d did not want Moses to blaze his own trail, carrying the people along on his back. G-d wanted the people to create the "inside" environment on their own. He wanted a system that would survive Moses and be effective in the long term. See *Likutei Sichot* XVI, p. 205.

"I feel conflicted between my drive to demand more from myself, as Moses did, and my need to take things slowly, as *Betzalel* advocated. Which is correct?"

MOSES, THE EXECUTIVE

THE ACHILLES' HEEL

Friends of mine, blessed with a wonderful marriage, recently confessed that money is the Achilles' heel of their relationship. He has always wanted to save and she has always wanted to spend. (They thought they were alone, huh?) It all boils down to he says/she says. He says that she spends every dime she gets; she says that he saves every penny he can. They visited a financial planner to settle the matter, and put the question bluntly before him, "Is it better to spend or to be thrifty?" His reply was, "Both."

TWO APPROACHES

Managing to keep a straight face, despite their look of dismay, he explained: "Every successful company employs a chief executive officer and a chief operations officer. The CEO formulates the overall mission, develops strategy, and identifies long-term goals. The COO is responsible for implementing strategy, while ensuring daily efficiency and maximum revenue. There is often tension between the two. The CEO is paid to view the company through the lens of its potential. The COO is paid to view the company from the perspective of its current capacity. The CEO sees the company as it ought to be whereas the COO sees the company as it actually is."

WORKING TOGETHER

"Both have a valid approach," the financial planner continued. "But because of their bias, each must be prepared to listen to the other. The CEO may well formulate a strategy that is completely beyond the company's true current capacity, in which case the COO must caution him to lower expectations and synchronize strategy with reality. On the other hand, the COO may well become so involved in the minutiae of implementation that he fails to see beyond the company's current capacity. In that case, the CEO must help him broaden his horizons and adjust accordingly. One can't see the trees for the forest; the other can't see the forest for the trees.

"For a company to succeed, each department must learn to appreciate the importance of the other. Goals cannot be met unless the company is fiscally healthy, yet fiscal health cannot be maintained without a successful long-term strategy. Each department must learn how to consider both angles.

"This," concluded the financial planner, "is the difference between your two approaches. Viewing each dollar through its investment potential is important to overall strategy and long-term financial viability. Viewing each dollar through its current purchasing capacity is vital for the household's department of operations. The key is to appreciate the value of both approaches and to communicate effectively."

MOSES AND AARON

As I listened to my friends' story, something clicked. For the first time, I understood something that had bothered me for many years. I had always wondered why G-d commanded that Moses and Aaron jointly lead the Children of Israel out of Egypt. Could Moses not have accomplished this on his own?[1]

When Moses first encountered G-d, at the Burning Bush, G-d told him to lead the Jewish People out of exile. He made no mention of Aaron. Only afterwards, when Moses repeatedly avoided the task, did G-d appoint Aaron as spokesperson for Moses.[2] But if Aaron was only a spokesperson, why is he accorded equal credit with Moses for the redemption?

POTENTIAL AND REALITY

At the time of their Exodus, the Jewish People were actually undeserving of salvation. They were an idolatrous nation, sunk to the lowest levels of impurity and depravity. But Moses, man of G-d, saw their innate capacity. He peered at them through the lens of their potential. He saw a people who would stand at Sinai and accept the Torah, willingly embracing its discipline — a people who could rise to the highest levels of ethical and spiritual

---

[1] *Exodus* 6:13 and 6:24.

[2] *Exodus* 3 and 4.

achievement. He saw the Jewish People through G-d's eyes, as it were, and positioned them on a trajectory that would help them realize this potential.

Wonderful as his view was, it had its drawbacks. When Moses encountered the nation's current reality, he saw petty impulses and depraved bickering, material cravings and empty temptation — and he didn't know how to respond. He couldn't relate to their base needs and human desires. In Moses' world, commitment to Torah and desire for G-d came naturally. Prompting was unnecessary and transgression unheard of. Moses knew that this was well within the potential of his People, but he realized that he couldn't actualize their potential by himself.

This is where Aaron came in. Aaron could relate to the People. He could understand their nature and character.

WORKING TOGETHER

G-d partnered Aaron with Moses so that Aaron would absorb Moses' exalted teachings and disseminate them to the people on a level that they could understand. Aaron was the "chief operations officer"; Moses was the "chief executive officer." Moses set forth the vision and strategy; Aaron was responsible for the implementation.[3]

Aaron knew what could be immediately expected from the People, and he knew what would require a little more patience. Aaron knew where to demand and where to suggest, where to insist and where to cajole. Moses set a furious pace: Aaron made certain the people could handle that pace. Moses led the nation on its journey to greatness. Aaron ensured a loving and gradual pace so that they remained committed to that journey.

MOSES AND AARON WITHIN

We are each endowed with a personal "Moses" and "Aaron," inside our mind and heart, who direct our focus. Our "Moses" drives us constantly

---

[3] This concept is adapted from an address given by Rabbi Menachem M. Schneerson, the Lubavitcher Rebbe in 1988.

forward, while our "Aaron" cautions us to slow down. Our "Moses" reminds us of all the *mitzvot* we have yet to accomplish, and urges us to strengthen our commitment. Our "Aaron" reminds us to set a steady pace and be wary of overdoing things.

In this interplay, we must first and foremost be honest with ourselves. There are times when our "Aaron" raises legitimate concerns and it is vital to set a more prudent, gradual pace. There are times when our "Moses" is right, when we must put aside our concerns and strike out courageously, following his lead.[4]

There is a Moses and Aaron within each of us. Moses supplies our lofty ambitions; Aaron keeps us in touch with the reality of what we are able to do right now. We must learn to listen to them both.

---

[4] This is in accordance with the teachings of the *Zohar*: "Moshe accompanies the King. Aaron accompanies the Bride" (*Zohar*, vol.1, ch. 266b). See also Likutei Torah, *Bamidbar* 2b and Likutei Sichot, vol 17, p. 113. This is also why we begin the Passover holiday with eating matzah, and continue from there to counting the Omer. Our Sages spoke of an association between grain and wisdom, "A child does not know to call his father till he eats his first piece of grain." Matzah is called "the poor man's bread." When eating matzah, we reflect humbly on the poverty of our understanding, and acknowledge our need for our teachers' guidance. In this sense, the teacher is Moses and the guidance he offers is the inspiration to improve our spiritual selves. The night of eating matzah is followed by the forty-nine-day count of the Omer, which symbolizes Aaron's gradual path of self-improvement. For more detail, see Torah Ohr 114b.

"We've discussed the need for constant growth — but isn't what looks like growth sometimes just a form of escapism? How can we know if we're seeking to move on because we're ready to grow, or if we're simply trying to get away from who and where we are?"

GENUINE GROWTH
TO TELL OR NOT TO TELL
When creating a resume or on a job interview, it's always hard to decide how many previous employments to list or mention. Listing many conveys an image of sophistication, but also a lack of stability. Listing only a few conveys an image of steady dependability, but also a lack of versatility.

Indeed, this is the very question we ponder when we consider changing our location or place of employment. Moving around prevents us from putting down roots and building on previous successes. On the other hand, staying in one place could result in missed opportunities. How do we balance these two important, but contradictory, considerations?

TWO PORTIONS
The name of a Torah portion reflects its general theme. When two portions are combined to be read on a single Shabbat, the combined names convey a common theme between the two portions. This rule presents a problem when we consider the Hebrew names of *Nitzavim* and *Vayelech,* two portions that are often read together on the same Shabbat. *Nitzavim* means to stand firmly, to remain firmly committed to one vocation or spot. *Vayelech* means to move forward; to seek out new possibilities. The two concepts seem contradictory; we cannot move forward and seek out new possibilities while remaining rooted to our original spot.

So it seems, at first glance, but as we probe the inner meaning of forward movement, a new understanding emerges. We discover that the two concepts are in fact compatible, even complementary.

In analyzing the two names, we notice the order in which they appear. First, *Nitzavim*; we commit ourselves to our original position. Then, after planting ourselves firmly in our original state, *Vayelech*, we permit ourselves to move forward and seek out new possibilities.

We must always examine our reasons for seeking new opportunities. Is it because I am generally discontent, unable to remain in one place for long? Or have I maximized my potential in my current career or location, with no room for further growth? The latter is an acceptable reason to relocate, the former is not. Only when we have maximized our potential in our current location is it appropriate to seek out new opportunities and move forward. At that point, remaining stationary causes stagnancy and complacency.

In the proper order, the two names complement each other, in their guidance of our deliberations. Only after we have maximized our *Nitzavim*, should we contemplate the possibility of V*ayelech*.

REVIEWING OUR RELATIONSHIPS

There are many ways to determine whether we generally tend to lay down roots, but one of the most effective ways is to examine the mindset with which we entered our current position and the attitude we maintained during our stay.

This too is reflected in the name of the Torah portion. *Nitzavim* means to stand firmly. The opening verse of this Torah portion records the words that Moses spoke to the nation: "You stand firmly today, together before G-d, your Lord — your leaders, tribal princes, water carriers, and wood hewers." Moses praised the nation for standing together as one entity — leaders and princes alongside children, proselytes, wood-hewers, and water-carriers. That they had integrated into a fully cohesive union demonstrated that *Nitzavim*, they were committed to and firmly rooted in their position.

When we move into a new community with the intention to lay down roots, we naturally reach out to form friendships and connections. When our stay is intended as temporary, we tend to shy away from deep bonds. "Why form bonds," we ask ourselves, "if they are not likely to last?"

A good way to measure the extent of our commitment to a community is to gauge our friendships within that community. If we have not developed genuine relationships with those around us, then we probably entered the community with a migratory mindset. We may not have realized that we carried this mindset, and of course it is possible that we simply never found anyone with whom we shared much in common. But all things being equal, normally balanced people usually find at least one or two candidates for friendship within a given community.

If we have developed genuine friendships, chances are that we were fully engaged in our community or vocation. If we now want to relocate, this probably stems from having maximized our potential in this community rather than because we never tried to make it work.

STATIONARY MOBILITY

What should we do if we realize that we never laid down firm roots and never really tried to make it work? Must we force ourselves to stay, even when our hearts want to leave? We are, of course, free to do as we please. However, we might consider remaining in place and satisfying our desire for mobility by introducing innovative ideas into our existing framework.

This too is implied by the juxtaposition of the two Torah portions. It is possible to achieve the enthusiasm and momentum of *Vayelech* (mobility) even when we remain *Nitzavim* (stationary). New horizons are not always found in new locations or places of employment. It is often possible to remain in our current position and find a novel approach that could stimulate us anew.

IN TORAH

When we resolve to grow in our practice of *mitzvot*, it is important to reflect on the patterns of our growth. Are we taking on a new mitzvah because we have grown bored with the *mitzvot* that we are already practicing? Or are we taking on a new mitzvah because we are genuinely ready for spiritual growth?

It is critical to understand the difference between the two and to distinguish spiritual growth from escapism. If our "growth" is a form of escaping the

REACHING FOR G-D

stagnation we feel with our current practice, it is destined to fail. Such "growth" is not lasting, and cannot resolve stagnation. With time, our new practice will also stagnate. Rather than focusing our attention on new observances, we must courageously face the problem that we are attempting to avoid, and correct it by stimulating new interest and infusing new passion into our religious practice.

On the other hand, it is equally important not to eschew all growth, under the pretext of avoiding escapism. When we are genuinely ready for spiritual growth, we must not delay. We must move forward with alacrity. Standing in the way of progress, invites the very stagnation that we seek to avoid.

Sometimes a fresh look at an old habit is all that's required for growth. But not always.

.

"It seems to me that all of these inspiring ideas were fine for our exalted ancestors. But in this modern age, are we capable of total devotion?

Total Devotion
The Burnt-Offering

Our ancestors offered many kinds of sacrifices: peace-offerings, sin-offerings, guilt-offerings, and also burnt-offerings. A burnt-offering is one that is burned in its entirety on the Altar. The Hebrew word for this offering is *Olah*, which means "ascent." The entire animal was placed atop the Altar. As the animal was physically raised to the Altar, so was it conceptually raised, when it was offered to G-d — from its animal state to a higher, more G-dly, state.

The Altar flames represent our passion for G-d. There is a raging fire within us — a fire of love and devotion. We are prepared to make sacrifices for G-d, because we love Him. The question is: how much are we prepared to sacrifice? The burnt-offering represents a total sacrifice.

In this modern age, are we capable of total devotion? Many Jews devote an hour to G-d in the morning. They attend synagogue, pray, study, and meditate. But when this hour is over, they return to their regular day. They feel that they have discharged their duty to G-d, and now reality beckons; they need to make a living or deal with their family and with life. They feel that, in ancient days, it was possible to rely on miraculous intervention; Jews were free to devote their entire day to Torah study. But today is different. They can afford to give G-d an hour — but a full day?

Is That All?

"This is the law of the burnt-offering. This is the burnt-offering ..."[1] Why does the verse repeat itself? The *Midrash* offers a parable: A king visited his friend and was greeted with dates and wine. The king was surprised, and asked, "Is that all you have prepared in my honor?" The friend replied,

---

[1] Leviticus 6:2.

"Your Majesty, this modest greeting is in the antechamber. Let's go into the parlor where the real feast awaits."

When G-d spoke of the burnt-offering, He commanded that it be offered every morning and evening. He then paused, as it were, and asked, "This is a burnt-offering?" Is one offering in the morning and one in the evening considered a total offering? This is only a partial offering! In today's age, when our prayers temporarily substitute for these offerings, we might ask, "Is an hour of prayer in the morning and an hour of study in the evening considered total devotion?"

Moses answered, "This is all we can bring in the antechamber. But when we enter the parlor, when the Moshiach comes, we will devote our day, fully and absolutely, to You. At that time we will have no earthly worries, for all will be provided from Above."[2]

TORAH STUDY

Nevertheless, even before Moshaich comes, there is an element of eternity to our moments of devotion. From *our* frame of reference, our devotion to G-d is only partial. But from *G-d's* frame of reference, even partial devotion can be a total offering. G-d transcends time; He created time. To G-d, every moment is forever. Our Sages taught that studying the laws of the burnt-offering in the Torah is tantamount to bringing a burnt-offering. It represents total devotion. This is because the study of Torah connects us to the Author of Torah — G-d — and from *His* frame of reference, every moment is forever.[3]

A moment of Torah study is eternal. These moments do not pass; they are never relegated to the waste bins of history. They are timeless. When our concentration is total and our focus complete, if only for a moment, we raise up a burnt-offering. A moment of absolute and complete ascent.[4]

---

[2] Yalkut Shimoni 479.

[3] *Babylonian Talmud, Menachot* 110a.

[4] See Tanya, ch. 25. See also ch. 29 and commentary of Rabbi Adin Steinsaltz.

ASHES

This is why every day of worship in the Temple began with collecting a handful of ashes from the sacrifices of the day before. In this way, our ancestors proclaimed that even intermittent worship is continuous. The last sacrifice was offered before sundown. There was a pause all night, while the priests rested. Nevertheless, today's offering is a continuation of yesterday's worship.

We may have needed to rest for several hours, but even as we left the Altar, our love for G-d did not abate. We pick up today from where we left off yesterday, for we are always devoted, always connected. No matter where we are, we stand before G-d. G-d is everywhere, in our homes as much as in the Temple. G-d exists in all times (or rather, all times exist in Him) at once. Yesterday exists before Him today as it did yesterday. This was the message of placing yesterday's ashes in front of today's offerings.

The Jew in the final generation bears responsibility for the very same mission borne by the Jew in the first generation. Ancestor and descendant share the same mandate. There may be a multi-generational gap; we may come from different ages and places. But the ashes proclaim that our mission is the same.[5]

HUMILITY

Constant devotion means a preparedness to obey every one of G-d commandments. Constant devotion means that we accept not only the *mitzvot* we enjoy very much, but also the ones we don't enjoy so much.

A seemingly trivial and menial task such as cleaning the ashes could have been relegated to a service staff rather than to the priests. Yet not only was this task given to the priests, they were commanded to fulfill it in full uniform. They performed their "janitorial duties" with the greatest pride. They were not concerned about soiling their vestments. If ashes fell on them — well these were holy ashes.

---

[5] Rabbi Samson Raphael Hirsch on *Leviticus* 6:3.

We, too, should not shy away from the commandments we might consider less important. Like the priests, we should relish such commandments, exult in the privilege and fulfill them with pride.

Such devotion is not possible without humility. Hence the requirement that the vestments be perfectly fitted to the priest. We must know our place. We must never presume to don a garment that is too large for us. We must never presume a level of piety that we have yet to achieve.[6]

THE LONG NIGHT

It is truly wondrous to realize that, on the Divine level, every moment lasts forever, and that any moment in which we do manage to serve Hashem will exist for all eternity. Nonetheless, we long to incorporate constant devotion into our own lives, on our own level. We long to achieve a burnt-offering even in our temporal sphere, where time (seems to) march on. We yearn to do that, but we need to be patient. We must wait for the Messianic era.

Though it has tarried we mustn't lose faith in its arrival. This is why the Torah specifies that the ashes be collected from fires that burned through the night, till the morning. Night is a metaphor for Exile; morning is a metaphor for Redemption. Throughout our long Exile, many fires have raged. Some have nearly consumed us, but we have survived. For we are protected by G-d.

The Torah assures us that, despite the conflagrations of the night, morning will yet dawn. Despite the incredible suffering that our people have endured during this terrible Exile, the Redemption will yet come.[7]

I believe with perfect faith in the coming of the Moshiach. And even though he has tarried, still I await him every day ... and meanwhile, even the smallest action I take in G-d's service can be complete and is, in any case, eternal.

---

[6] Kli Yakar and Rabbeinu Bachya on *Leviticus* 6:3.

[7] Kli Yakar and Or HaChayim on *Leviticus* 6:2.

Part Two – The Soul's Bond With G-d

"When I hear or read about serving G-d, it's all very inspiring. But the reality is that I am where and who I am. And I know only too well that it's not good. Does that mean that G-d hates me? Is He barely tolerating me? And how can I, where and who I am right now, experience any kind of a bond with him?"

Sounds of Silence

The Meaning of Sound

Life is filled with audible indicators, and we find them reassuring. In the office, it's the constant hum of the computer. In the supermarket, it's the steady buzz of conversation. At home, it's the sounds of children at play. These sounds are woven into the very fabric of life; they reassure us that all is running smoothly. Even as the incessant honking of traffic drives us crazy, even as we crave a moment's peace, we find the noise comforting. Should those little sounds ever stop purring, we would crave these most elementary indicators of life.

Even in repose, there is mild activity. Even in stillness, there is slight movement. Even in quiet, there is muted sound. When I imagine serenity, I conjure up images of gentle breezes, and softly lapping waves. I think of floating yachts, coasting seagulls, and shimmering rays of sunlight. These may be tranquil, placid movements and soft sounds, but they are movement and sound nonetheless.

A Time for Silence

The absence of sound may be comforting for a moment of two, but, long-term, it is *too* silent for our tastes. Before long, we feel compelled to flee. We call a friend, turn on the radio — anything to escape the oppressive stillness of silence. Beyond life, spans a vast stillness. When all is achieved and activity has ceased, when there is nothing to strive for and nothing to attain, then we will be afforded silence. There will be plenty of time for that silence. For now, we prefer our silences punctuated by the pulsing sounds of life.

Sound means activity, activity means movement, and movement means progress to bridge the gap, the discrepancy between where we are and where we want to be. When we arrive at our ultimate destination, we can afford to lie low, but life is not the time for that. Life is a time for momentum, for forward thrust, for expansion, and for growth.

THE JINGLING BELLS

This affinity for sound may help to explain why the *KohenKohen Gadol*, the High Priest, was commanded to wear bells on the hem of his tunic.[1] The bells jingled softly as he walked; they announced his presence ahead of his entrance.[2]

At first glance, this seems a curious intrusion. Is not the House of G-d best served by dignity and quiet decorum? Don't these sounds draw undue attention to the High Priest and detract from our focus on G-d?

If drawing attention to the High Priest were the purpose of the bells, these would indeed be questions. But this was not their purpose. These bells reflected the essence of life. They represented the hustle and bustle of movement and growth. The High Priest did not live in a vacuum of spiritual seclusion. He lived in a world where ordinary people struggled to forge an extraordinary relationship with G-d. In this struggle, ordinary people are often found wanting. Despite our best efforts, we know we can do better. We find ourselves growing on a curve; caught up in a momentum of upward mobility; we always desire more. This movement is reflected in the soft jingling of the bells.

The High Priest raised ordinary Jews aloft, by serving as their inspiration to climb ever higher. As he advanced through the Temple's sacred corridors, the call of his bells summoned ordinary people to escape the mundane, to rise from below to above and to find spiritual inspiration.

---

[1] *Exodus* 28:33.

[2] *Exodus* 28:35.

A HOLY SILENCE

There was, however, one day in the year when the High Priest shed his tunic with its dangling bells. This was Yom Kippur, the holiest day of the year when he entered the holiest Chamber in the Temple. When he entered G-d's Chamber, he was silent. No bells marked his advance. No sounds announced his entry.[3]

The question begs itself. Why not? Is not utter silence the mark of death? Can anything be more alive than G-d Himself? Should not our presence before Him be marked by the ultimate sounds of life?

The answer lies in the nature of that Chamber. This was not the High Priest's chamber. This was G-d's Chamber. In this room, the High Priest did not think of himself, of where he was, or of where he would like to be. He did not think of other Jews, of where they were, or of where they would like to be. This room was not about people. It was about G-d. Here, mortals were silent. This was not the silence of a vacuum, but of utter selflessness. It was the silence of a surrendering ego and a complete merging with G-d.

Once our egos are surrendered, and we are merged with G-d, we have no further need to ascend. Our scale of spiritual growth notwithstanding, we have touched the Divine. This is the pinnacle; scaling another peak cannot draw us higher. G-d is here just as He is there, lower just as He is higher. We have discovered G-d and G-d is everywhere.

On Yom Kippur we arrive at the essence. There are no further goals to reach. There is no need for mobility, activity, or sound. There is only silence. Sound has not been suspended; it has been transcended.[4]

Yom Kippur reminds us that G-d is everywhere, in the lowest places as in the highest, and that G-d's love for us, and His bond with us, is just as real where we are right now.

---

[3] *Torat Kohanim* on Exodus 16, 4. However, see footnote 18 in the sichah for further analysis.

[4] This essay is largely based on Likutei Sichot XVI p. 336.

"It's good to know that our bond with G-d transcends our personal growth. Is that bond intrinsic? Are we born with it? Can it also stimulate our spiritual growth?"

THE POWER OF CIRCUMCISION
THREE GIFTS
The mitzvah of circumcision promises three rewards: manifestation of the Divine Presence, eternal ownership of the Land of Israel, and preservation of the patrilineal line of Davidic descent.[1] We can easily understand that, as a seal of the covenant between G-d and the Jewish People, circumcision is rewarded by a manifestation of the Divine Presence among us. But what is there in the nature of circumcision that leads to ownership of the Land of Israel? And to the preservation of David's line? To understand why circumcision leads to these specific gifts, it is first necessary to better understand circumcision itself.

DIVINE MANIFESTATION
"And on the eighth day, the flesh of his foreskin shall be circumcised."[2] The requirement of circumcision at the tender age of eight days raises an important question: Why is the eternal covenant of Divine manifestation granted to an infant, who is completely oblivious to its significance? Furthermore, how can we know if the infant will ever learn to appreciate this significance? Shouldn't we wait till he has demonstrated at least a modicum of commitment, before we bestow such a gift on him?

EXPERIENTIAL AND INTRINSIC
We, the Jewish People are connected to G-d on two separate levels: the experiential and the intrinsic.[3]

---

[1] Rabbeinu Bachya on *Genesis* 17:24.

[2] Our Parshah, *Leviticus* 12:3.

[3] For a full treatment of this subject, see Likutei Sichot XXV, p. 87. See also Machshevet Hachassidut, vol. 1, p. 93.

The experiential bond is the relationship we form through our observance of His commandments. This bond is determined by our devotion. The greater our passion for G-d, the more we will want to seek Him out. The greater our yearning for G-d, the more committed we will be to His commandments. On this level, we fulfill His commandments because we love Him and pine for closeness to Him. Every commandment is a channel for connection, and every transgression is the blocking of a channel. The intensity of this bond de-depends completely on us. We can build it or we can sever it.

The intrinsic bond works in the reverse. G-d binds Himself to our essence, thereby forging an intrinsic connection with us. This bond is inescapable. Whether we are cognizant of it or oblivious to it, we and G-d are forever one. This bond is unchanging. Our sins don't diminish it; our *mitzvot* don't enhance it. It is a bond with the Infinite, and Infinity is unchanging. The pious and the wicked, the honest and the corrupt, the scholar and the simpleton are intrinsically and identically bound to G-d.

The experiential bond is our connection with G-d. The intrinsic bond is G-d's connection with us. While we might terminate our relationship with G-d, G-d never terminates his relationship with us.

It is this intrinsic bond that is reflected in the circumcision's covenant of Divine manifestation. [4] The covenant is deliberately administered during infancy *because* the infant is completely oblivious to the magnitude of its im-

---

[4] The Torah speaks of two forms of circumcision, the physical and the spiritual. In addition to the conventional form of circumcision, the Torah instructs us to "circumcise the foreskin of our hearts" (*Deuteronomy* 10:16). This means to restrain our passion for worldly delights and direct our focus exclusively on G-d. Devotees of such circumcision perfect their experiential bond with G-d. Yet the *Midrash* teaches that G-d's instruction to Abraham to attain a state of wholeness was made possible only through physical circumcision, not through the spiritual circumcision of the heart. This indicates that the mitzvah of circumcision is related primarily to our intrinsic bond with G-d. See *Bereishit Rabbah* 46:5.

pact. The infant's cognizance is immaterial to the intrinsic bond. It could not be enhanced by his allegiance, nor could it be diminished by his perfidy.[5]

THE LAND OF ISRAEL

The prophet Isaiah wrote of the Holy Land: "As a young man espouses a maiden, so shall your children settle in you; and like the bridegroom's rejoicing over his bride, so shall your G-d rejoice over you."[6]

Isaiah is saying that our presence in the Land of Israel forms a bond with G-d that is similar to the marital bond between a bride and groom. The marital bond is experiential. The bride and groom have no intrinsic love for each other; they aren't joined at their essence. Their love will grow out of and fluctuate with their marriage. As their marriage flourishes, so does their love. Whenever their love wanes, so does their marriage. This fluctuating love is analogous to our experiential bond with G-d, which fluctuates with our commitment. The environment of the Land of Israel enhances our commitment in ways that are not possible elsewhere.

A Jew in Israel is spiritually more attuned to inspiration. The Torah can be fully appreciated and understood only in the Land of Israel.[7] Many of the Torah's commandments are applicable only in the Land of Israel.[8] With the

---

[5] This may explain the *Midrashic* teaching that the mitzvah of circumcision atones for all sins and protects one from passage to *Gehinnom*. See *Bereishit Rabbah* 21:9, 47:7, and 48:7; *Shemot Rabbah* 19:4; *Pirkei Rebbe Eliezer* 29. This may also explain why our Sages equate the sanctity and devotion of a Jew during circumcision with that of a sacrifice at the time of its offering. See *Bereishit Rabbah* 25:4; *Babylonian Talmud, Sanhedrin* 89b.

[6] *Isaiah* 63:5.

[7] *Yalkut Shimoni*, Genesis 22: "There is no Torah like the Torah of Israel and there is no wisdom like the wisdom of Israel." See also *Babylonian Talmud, Baba Metzia* 85a. Rabbi *Zeira*, a Talmudic Sage, fasted for one hundred days before he moved from Babylon to Israel, so that he would merit to forget the lesser level of Torah study available in the Diaspora and attain the higher level of Torah study available in Israel.

[8] Commandments related to agriculture, such as *shmittah*, *trumah*, and *maasrot*.

exception of Moses, every one of our prophets lived, at least for a while, in the Holy Land. This Land opens many lines of connection that are simply not available in the Diaspora. These lines of connection are the life force of our experiential bond.[9]

Though the intrinsic and experiential bonds are independent of each other, they nevertheless affect each other. When our intrinsic bond is manifested through circumcision, our experiential bond is strengthened. We thus explain why the Land of Israel, reflective of the experiential bond, is promised to us as a reward for the mitzvah of circumcision.

THE DAVIDIC LINE OF DESCENT

Jewish tradition teaches that the Messiah, in Hebrew "*Moshiach*," will be a direct patrilineal descendant of King David.[10] For the Jewish Messianic hope to stay alive and be fulfilled, it is vital that this patrilineal line be preserved. Thus the preservation of this line is the final reward for the mitzvah of circumcision. The first reward, Divine manifestation, promises an intrinsic bond with G-d. The second reward, ownership of the Land of Israel, promises an experiential bond with G-d. The third reward, patrilineal line of Davidic descent, promises to merge the two bonds.

Our prophets describe the Messianic era as a time when the human eye will gaze on G-d's very Essence.[11] Human vision is a metaphor for our experiential bond with G-d, because like that bond, its range is finite. It is possible to gaze on a moderate intensity of light; with effort, the pupil expands and we increase the range of our capacity. But it is impossible to gaze directly on an intense source of light such as the sun. Yet the Messianic prophecy promises that the capacity of the human eye will extend to the point of gazing directly on G-d's very Essence, a Source of light that infinitely transcends the light of

---

[9] For more information on the symbiotic relationship between the Jewish People and the Land of Israel, see *Rectifying the State of Israel* by Rabbi Yitzchak Ginsburgh.

[10] *Yad Hachazakah, Hilchot Melachim* 11:4.

[11] *Isaiah* 30:20.

the sun, yet we will not be overwhelmed. Circumcision and the Land of Israel make this possible.[12]

Circumcision enhances our intrinsic bond; the Land of Israel enhances our experiential bond. The former strengthens our connection to G-d's Essence; the latter strengthens our capacity to relate to finite expressions of Divinity. When our bond with G-d succeeds on both levels, we become highly sensitized to our spiritual capacity, and thus deserving of the third and greatest reward: the preservation of the Davidic line — the Messianic prophecy, which will merge the two bonds. Indeed, when the *Moshiach* comes, we will merit an *experiential* bond with G-d's very *essence*.

Our intrinsic bond does indeed stimulate spiritual growth. This will be most manifest when the Moshiach comes. It is for this reason that the Prophets and Sages all yearned for Moshiach. Aso do we.

---

[12] Settlement of the Land of Israel is itself a harbinger of the *Moshiach*, as the following quote demonstrates: "Settlement of all parts of the Land of Israel will affect the nations, to the extent that they will assist us. They will also 'feel' that the existence of Esau is only for the purpose of helping Jacob. This will be a preparation for the ingathering of all of Israel — *shleimut haAm* — to the whole of the Land of Israel, in the coming of (and through) *Moshiach*, after which 'G-d will extend your boundaries' — and the Land of Israel will be expanded, with the addition of the lands of the *Keini, Knizi,* and *Kadmoni*." (Quoted from an address by Rabbi Menachem M. Schneersohn, the Lubavitcher Rebbe, , on Motzaei *Shabbat* Chayei Sarah, 5738.)

"I see how my soul is intrinsically bound to G-d. Can you suggest concrete ways of expressing this holy bond?"

EXCLUSIVE DEDICATION

SANCTITY AND DEDICATION

Among the many commandments of the Torah, one stands out, with its clarion call to spiritual transcendence: "Be holy," the Torah commands us. "For I [G-d] am holy."[1] How does one sanctify oneself? What does the Torah mean when it tells us that G-d is holy? Why does the fact that G-d is holy require holiness of us?

"Kedushah," the Hebrew word for sanctity, also means betrothal. For millennia, Jews have established matrimony with the words, "Thou are hereby sanctified unto me." How does a bride become sanctified to a bridegroom? To be sanctified means to be dedicated. Dedication means exclusion. The bride separates herself from all others, and dedicates herself to her bridegroom alone. In this sense the bridegroom is also sacred, for he too has undertaken to separate himself from all other women and has dedicated himself to his bride alone.

We cannot be truly dedicated to any one cause until we are fully divested from all other causes. We can be partially dedicated to many causes, but we can be fully dedicated to only one cause.

THE EXCLUSIVE G-D

The commandment to sanctify ourselves is a commandment to dedicate ourselves. To Whom? To G-d, who is Himself holy. G-d is transcendent; separated from all worldliness. If we want to bond with G-d, we must first transcend all worldly considerations. This is one fence that cannot be strad-

---

[1] *Leviticus* 19:1.

dled. One can either be on the worldly side or on G-d's side, but one cannot be on both sides at once. [2]

When we make space for G-d, there can be no space left for others; and if we have reserved space for others, then there is not enough space left for G-d. Of course, G-d is also patient. If He can't have all of us today, he is prepared to wait until we are ready. But He will not settle for less than our complete self.

ALL THINGS PERMITTED

Our Sages took this commandment to a whole new level, when they interpreted it in the following way: "Sanctify yourself," they said, "with that which is otherwise permitted to you." In plain words, this means that we must separate ourselves even from those pursuits that are permitted to us by Jewish Law. There is no question that we must divest ourselves from that which is forbidden by Jewish Law, but G-d wants more than that. He wants us to surrender even those little pleasures that He has permitted us. If G-d has permitted them, what can be wrong with them?

There is nothing wrong with the items that are permitted, but there is something wrong with our indulgence in those items. We cannot indulge ourselves and immerse ourselves in G-dliness at the same time. This is not about separating the permitted *pleasures* from ourselves; it is about separating *ourselves* from those pleasures. If our incentive for a particular pursuit is personal, rather than G-dly, then indulgence of that pursuit is an exercise in self-pleasure, which precludes dedication to the Divine, at that moment.

Let's consider, by way of example, the desire to go on vacation. This desire contains two distinct points: the desire itself and the object of the desire, namely the vacation.

Both points must be examined, so let us begin with the object of the desire. The vacation is appropriate only if all the factors connected to it are as they

---

[2] See Sifra on *Leviticus* 11:44: "Just as I am holy, so shall you be holy." See also Ramban on *Leviticus* 19:1. Finally see Tanya, ch. 27.

should be. Are we trying to escape something at home? Can we afford a vacation at this time? Will we be able to obey the dietary and ethical Torah laws, during our vacation? If all the factors are as they should be, the vacation is appropriate. If they aren't, neither is the vacation.

Having determined that the object of the desire is appropriate, let us now examine the desire itself, the fact that I have a desire. Here we come to the crux of the matter. Is it okay to desire? In other words, is it right for us to make so much of ourselves that we feel driven to fulfill our desires merely because we desire them?

Separation from Self

If we want to be truly dedicated to G-d, then we must be fully sanctified, fully divested from all other pursuits, including pursuit of ourselves and our desires. We must take ourselves completely out of the equation, because we cannot be dedicated to self and to G-d at the same time.[3]

This doesn't mean that we must deny ourselves all permitted things. It means that we should be wary of making too much of our own desires. We should not fulfill our desires merely because we desire them. We must first ask ourselves if G-d will be served though this permitted thing. If the answer is yes, the permitted thing is a mitzvah for us, not because we wanted it, but because G-d will be served through it. If the answer is no, we should either hold off or find new ways to integrate our indulgence and our service to G-d.

How can we know if G-d could be served through this permitted thing? In our heart of hearts, we all know the answer to that. If there are more important places we could be, or more important things we should do, then it is better that we wait and put off this permitted thing for some other time.

---

[3] G-d says of the arrogant, "He and I cannot dwell together in the same world." We cannot occupy the space that another is already occupying. If we leave space for G-d, He is "free" to occupy it. If we take it for ourselves, G-d is "denied" access to that space. Hence, G-d says, "He and I cannot dwell in the same space," and, as it were, removes Himself.

In Conclusion

G-d says, "Sanctify yourself." Our Sages say, "Separate yourself from the things permitted to you." We need not deny ourselves that which is permitted to us. We need only separate ourselves from them and do them for reasons greater than ourselves.

The exclusively dedicated don't ask themselves if they want to go on vacation; they ask themselves if G-d wants them to go. Exclusive dedication is a tall order. However, in light of our intrinsic bond with G-d, we can all strive for at least a measure of such dedication. We definitely have the soul power to achieve it. All that remains is to develop the will.

"There are certain *mitzvot* about which we are told that they are designed to further enhance our bond with G-d. The mitzvah of shmittah is one such example. How does it do this?"

THE POWER OF WHAT

SABBATICAL

Farmers in Israel are commanded by the Torah to work their land for six years and let it lie fallow on the seventh. But when all the fields in a country are permitted to lie fallow for an entire year, would that nation not face a very real risk of famine? In the following verse the Torah addresses this concern: "And if you shall ask, 'What will we eat in the seventh year?' I shall ordain my blessing on the sixth year and it will yield a crop sufficient for the three-year period."[1]

The Torah does not usually articulate the questions; it simply provides the answers. What can we learn from the fact that the Torah asks this particular question?[2]

SOCIETAL MORALITY

Society at large lives by a moral code. Governments legislate against immoral behavior, such as murder and theft, and encourage ethical behavior, such as charity and modesty. If you were to ask why murder is forbidden, the curt response would probably be, "Because taking another person's life is just plain *wrong*." If you were to persist and ask, "But *why* is it wrong?" the answer might very well be, "Because it *is*!" If you were to further ask what

---

[1] *Numbers* 25:20–21. The three-year period encompasses the sixth, seventh, and eighth year, since the nation must be sustained till the eighth year's crop is harvested.

[2] Not only is it curious that the Torah asks the question, but the manner of articulation is curious too. Though we used literary license with the translation and quoted the verse as "If you shall *ask*," the Torah uses the words, "... if you shall *say*, 'What will we eat?'" but since this is a question, the Torah should have stated, "...if you shall *ask* what I eat?". Yet the verse appears to be a statement presented as a question. (See footnote 7.)

REACHING FOR G-D

makes it so, you could expect to hear something like, "If you don't sense it intuitively, then there's no point in trying to explain it to you." This would indeed be the correct answer. Society intuitively senses the immoral nature of murder.

DIVINE MORALITY

If you ask a Jew why murder is wrong, he or she is likely to reply, "Because it's one of the Ten Commandments!" If you persist and ask *why* it is one of the Ten Commandments, the answer would likely be, "That's G-d's Will. Do you expect to understand the Divine?" Jews, too, intuitively sense the inherent immorality of murder, but to a Jew it is more than mere intuition. Since G-d commanded this prohibition, it must be immoral, for reasons beyond human intuition.

BEYOND THE HUMAN MIND

Why does a Jew believe that Divine commandments are beyond human intuition?

Mitzvot are generally divided into two categories: ethical commandments that are easily understood, and inexplicable decrees that defy our comprehension. The prohibition of theft is an example of the former, and the law of the Red Heifer is an example of the latter.

The ethical commandments and the inexplicable decrees are symbiotically related, each affecting the way we view the other. The ethical commandments demonstrate that it is possible to gain a modicum of understanding of G-d's commandments. The decrees demonstrate that, in the final analysis, G-d's wisdom infinitely exceeds our own.[3]

If we had been given only the decrees, our lack of understanding would have alienated us from the commandments. We would be unable to identify with them or to muster enthusiasm for them. On the other hand, if we had been given only the ethical commandments, we would have assumed that all Di-

---

[3] *Yad hachazakah, Hilchot Me'ilah*, ch. 8. *Hilchot Temurah*, ch. 4.

vinity is within the grasp of human comprehension. This might have impelled us to dismiss matters of faith that lie beyond our understanding. The inexplicable decrees teach the Jew to view even the easily understood commandments through the prism of Divine wisdom, and to recognize that even ethical commandments, such as the prohibition of murder, are beyond our cognitive or intuitive grasp.[4]

TWO QUESTIONS – ONE WORD

This is the meaning of the question, asked in the Passover *Haggadah*, by the wise son: "What are the ... decrees and [ethical] commandments that G-d our Lord has commanded you?"[5] The wise son understands that even the easily understood commandments have dimensions that defy human comprehension, and so he asks to understand the true meaning of all the mitzvah categories; not just the decrees — the [ethical] commandments, too.

We now return to the question posed in our original verse, "If you shall ask, 'What will we eat in the seventh year?' ... " The only other question in the entire Torah that is introduced with the words, "And if you shall ask" is that of one of the four sons: "And if your son shall ask ... " It can therefore be assumed that the question about the seventh year is also asked by one of the four sons.

---

[4] This explains why the Psalmist says, "He spoke ... his decrees and mishpatim to Israel. He has done so for no other nation; and of His *mishpatim*, He has not informed them." According to our understanding, the word "*mishpatim*" refers to ethical commandments. (*Psalms* 147:19–20) One wonders why the Psalmist prides himself on being a member of the only nation to receive G-d's ethical commandments. Is it not true that, even without receiving these commandments, most other nations have taken on these ethical precepts? But it is not the commandments themselves that the Psalmist is proud of; it is our approach to their reasons. The nations of the world accept these ethical standards because of reasons that they intuitively grasp, but they ascribe no exalted wisdom to them. A Jew relates to the ethical standards as a sacred decree that contains secrets concealed in the realm of the Divine.

[5] *Deuteronomy* 6: 20.

Which of the four sons is likely to ask this question? It is safe to assume that it is the wise son. This question is cited in the Torah only after all the laws of the Sabbatical are first outlined. We thus deduce that this question is asked by the wise son, who has studied the entire subject and who is left with but one question.[6]

The wise son's questions are quoted twice in the Torah: "What is the meaning … " and "What shall we eat … " Though the questions seem unrelated, there is one word that connects them. The word "What."

THE MEANING OF WHAT

The Jewish People are accustomed to this word. We always ask questions: *What* is the reason? *What* is the meaning? Like the wise son, we ask this question about all commandments and all events, even those we supposedly understand. We realize that, in the final analysis, our comprehension doesn't capture the Divine thought.

What is not only a question. It is also a statement. Because, in the end, the question must be allowed to stand unanswered. The *what* acknowledges our lack of understanding, and asks G-d for His true reason, but we don't claim entitlement to His answer. We plumb the Heavenly secrets to the extent that the human mind is capable, but the rest is humbly left to G-d. The word *what* demonstrates profound humility. We ask it not in quarrel, but in acceptance. We ask it not in arrogance, but in submission. We ask it not in confusion, but in serene faith.

"*What* shall we eat in the seventh year," is not a question as much as a statement: "In the seventh year, we shall eat *what(ever)*." We don't know *what* the sabbatical year will bring, but we are not concerned about a famine, either. We humbly and confidently place our trust in G-d.[7]

---

[6] Likutei Sichot, vol. 27, p. 185. Furthermore, in its introduction, the *Haggadah* text draws special attention to the word "*what*": "The wise son, *what* does he say?"

[7] We now also understand why the Torah uses the words, " … if you shall *say*." Not, "… if you shall *ask*" (see footnote 2). This is not a question as much as it is a

This is also why the Torah articulates this question. The way this question is stated is precisely what precipitates the answer. We ask *what*. We proclaim that we don't know what we might eat; and in the same breath, we acknowledge that we are not worried, because we trust G-d. The Torah assures us that G-d will not remain indebted, if we approach this mitzvah with the humility prescribed by the word *what*. He will command His blessing on the sixth year, and it will yield a crop sufficient for all three years.[8]

Sometimes (if not all times) the human brain is too small to figure out all the answers. At such times (if not all times), our worries are best left to G-d. The mitzvah of shmittah forces us to cultivate our faith in G-d and to trust Him to provide. Such trust is not easily cultivated, but once achieved, life is immeasurably enhanced.

---

statement of fact. We don't know what we will eat, but we trust that we *will* eat. It is interesting to note that the *Haggadah* also uses the same expression: "The wise son, what does he *say*?" not "What does he *ask*?"

[8] For more detail on this concept, see Sefer Be'er Mayim Chayim on this verse.

"So the main thing is just to pray to G-d about everything, and then to trust Him, right? If so, why do I have to do anything?"

OVERCOMING OBSTACLES
PARTING WATERS
Behind the Jewish camp was an army, bristling for the kill. Before them was an ocean, deep and impassable. They could neither advance nor retreat. They were ambushed. What could they do? Moses tried an age-old tactic. He cried to G-d.

But G-d rebuked him: "Why do you cry to me? Tell the Children of Israel to journey forth."[1]

Journey forth. But how? There was an ocean before them! G-d never addressed this question, and Moses never asked it. G-d said to journey forth and journey forth they did. That was the entire point. Don't ask questions. Don't raise doubts. If G-d issues a command, He will provide the means to see it through.

Yet the Children of Israel hesitated. They were prepared to plow into the ocean, but they needed to be led. And a leader appeared, in the person of *Nachson*, son of *Aminadav*, tribal prince of Judah. Leading his tribal column, *Nachshon* strode into the raging sea. Wading through the rising tide, he felt the waters reach his waist, then his chest, then his shoulders. Determined to obey G-d's command, *Nachshon* doggedly advanced, and was almost overcome by the surging waters. At the very last moment, as the waters reached his nostrils, the Reed Sea parted, and the Children of Israel followed him into the sea.[2]

Why Did the Waters Part?

---

[1] *Exodus* 14:15.

[2] See *Mechilta* 14:22, *Midrash Tehillim* 114:8, and *Bamidbar Rabbah* 13:7. See also Radak on *Tehillim* 114:2. See, however, Rabbeinu Bachya on *Exodus* 14:15, that all the tribes competed for the privilege of being first, and *Nachshon*, leading the tribe of Judah, triumphed. See also the two opinions in *Sotah* 37a.

The *Midrash* cites many reasons for which our ancestors merited the Splitting of the Sea. According to at least one of our Sages, the waters parted because of our ancestors' profound faith and unwavering confidence that G-d would protect them.[3]

All created beings are subject to change. Winds blow, waters flow, vegetation grows, even stones are worn down. Man, too, is subject to change. The only Constant in our ever-changing world is G-d.[4] There is, however, one phenomenon in the universe that manifests the unchanging nature of the Divine and that is our unshakable and unchanging faith in G-d. A Jew who demonstrates undying faith and absolute trust in G-d emulates G-d's unchanging nature. When we believe, we reflect the unchanging character of the Divine.

When our ancestors approached the waters with implicit faith in G-d, the waters glimpsed in them this reflection of the Divine. The created being, the waters, could not stand in the path of that which reflected its Creator, the People; the waters had to part. As our ancestors approached with intention to pass, the waters, instinctively and spontaneously, receded before those who were emulations of their Creator.[5]

WHY NOW?

The question is not why the waters parted, but why the waters waited till *Nachshon* performed his act of brinkmanship.

The waters waited for the Jews to *express* their faith, their bond with G-d, through *action*. It was not enough that Jews believed; the sea demanded a demonstration of their faith. Faith is a quality of the soul, which exists within us at all times. Even when we deny our faith, our soul within, bound to G-d, continues to believe. G-d, however, is not satisfied with our soul's dormant

---

[3] *Mechilta* on *Exodus* 14:15. *Shemos Rabbah* 23:5. See also Rashi on *Exodus* 14:15.

[4] Gevurot Hashem, ch. 8 and 40.

[5] King David wrote in Psalm 114: "The ocean saw and fled." What did it see, and from whom did it flee? It saw Divinity reflected in Moses's raised arm and it fled from being an obstacle in G-d's path. See *Bamidbar Rabbah* 21:6.

faith, because such faith has no impact on the physical world. He challenges us to fan the flames of our ever-present, but silent, faith, and to express it, actualize it, through physical action. Only when *Nachshon* sallied forth, giving external expression and actualization to his inner faith, would the waters finally part.[6]

TOTAL DEVOTION

Every Jew is capable of reaching the pinnacle of devotion that *Nachshon* reached at that moment. When a Jew performs G-d's Will with resolve, and with total disregard for the obstacles, G-d provides a way to overcome the obstacles. When we are absolutely determined to keep Shabbat, G-d shows us a way to make it possible. When we are absolutely committed to don tefillin (phylacteries), G-d shows us a way to make it happen. When we are absolutely committed to walk in the path of Torah, G-d grants us the strength to do so. Like the Reed Sea, our obstacles flee, to allow us clear and unimpeded passage.

There is a Nachshon in every one of us. Our task is to find it in the recesses of our soul and summon it to action.

---

[6] Tanya, ch. 45. See also Magid Devarav L'Yaakov 261, for an explanation on why meditation is not sufficient in prayer. Note the link explained there between actual oral articulation of prayer and the Splitting of the Sea of Reeds.

"I see why, in times of need or difficulty, such as during *shmittah*(Sabbatical Year), it is important to trust G-d. But what role does faith play in times of prosperity?"

THE MONEY TRAP
FORGETTING G-D

Moses was atop Mount Sinai, but he was already expected to have arrived back at the camp below. When he failed to return at the designated time, the People worried that G-d might have taken him. Afraid that he might never return, they asked Aaron to create a new material god.[1] Aaron was appalled. A new G-d? It was barely forty days since G-d, the Creator of Heaven and earth had expressly forbidden worship of false gods. Had they so quickly forgotten?

Aaron was then struck by a sudden insight. The cause of this sudden betrayal must have been the fabulous wealth that the people had been granted before their Exodus from Egypt. People of wealth are accustomed to having their every desire fulfilled, and they quickly learn to feel entitled. The people wanted a material god and, in their arrogance, felt entitled to one. If a problem would present itself, they were prepared to solve it with money. Don't all problems solve themselves when "palms are greased" with appropriate sums?[2]

With this insight into the people's motivation, Aaron attempted to address the root of the problem. He asked them, "Who owns gold?" He had planned to explain that all gold comes from G-d, and that when we merit wealth we ought to be humbled by G-d's generosity. He intended to encourage them to

---

[1] *Exodus* 32.

[2] See Rashi on *Deuteronomy* 1:1 that the Sin of the Golden Calf was a direct result of their fabulous wealth. See also *Deuteronomy* 8:11–18.

meditate on this concept, thinking that such meditation might solve the underlying cause of the problem.[3]

THROWING MONEY AT THE PROBLEM

But Aaron never got a chance to finish his thought. As soon as he asked for gold, the People rejoiced. If money was all that stood between them and a new god, they would have a new god in no time. They had plenty of gold, and arrogantly brought forth a huge amount.[4]

What was Aaron to do? At this point, it was too late for words. The radical situation called for decisive action. He threw the gold into the fire. By this he meant to communicate that all gold comes from Heaven and that wealth ought to fuel the flames of our love for G-d, rather than the reverse. To his chagrin, it was too late. The people's attitude was so corroded, it would not change overnight. As Aaron later testified, "I threw the gold into the fire and out came this Calf." The very image of gold glistening and shimmering in the fire stoked the nation's passion for money. The fire gave birth to a Golden Calf. And because they had paid for it, they arrogantly claimed title to it, proclaiming, "This is your god, O Israel!" Your god, as in the god that belongs to you.

WHEN THE "I" IS PARAMOUNT

On his descent from the mountain, Moses perceived this immediately. He told his student, Joshua, who awaited him at the foot of the mountain, "This is not a sound of victory, this is not a sound of defeat, this is a sound of blas-

---

[3] This essay follows Aaron's account of his exchange with the People. Aaron reported to Moses (*Exodus* 32:44) that all he had said to the People was, "Who has gold?" In the account of the event itself, the Torah tells us that Aaron actually said, "Remove your rings of gold that are on your wives, sons, and daughters, and bring them to me" (32:2). Aaron was, of course, paraphrasing when he reported to Moses, but even the longer version of Aaron's words can be interpreted in the same manner. Aaron said, "Remove your sense of ownership from the gold. You gave it to your family as if you are entitled to it. Bring it to me and I will show you how to treat the blessing of wealth appropriately."

[4] Divrei Yisrael al Hatorah.

phemy I hear."[5] Why did he conclude his statement with the seemingly superfluous words, "I hear?" According to at least one commentator, Moses was telling Joshua that the source of the blasphemy was an inflated sense of self. Their arrogant sense of "I" stimulated a sense of entitlement, which ultimately resulted in blasphemy and idolatry.[6]

This problem of wealth sparking arrogance has plagued humanity through history. All too often, the wealthy live in exclusive communities and are accustomed to having their every wish fulfilled. They rarely interact with lower-income classes; they prefer the rarefied echelons. How do we solve this problem and protect ourselves against the pitfalls of wealth? We take further inspiration from the second half of the Biblical tale.

A MESSAGE OF HUMILITY
When G-d consented to grant the second set of Tablets, He told Moses to carve Tablets from a sapphire quarry that was created especially for this purpose, inside Moses' tent. When G-d told him to carve out the Tablets, he added the word "lecha," which means, "for yourself." Carve out for yourself.[7]

The Tablets didn't belong to Moses; they were the heritage of the entire nation. Why did G-d tell Moses to carve them out for himself? The Hebrew word for carve is "psal," which also means "inferior (stone-dust.)" G-d was not telling Moses that the Tablets belonged to him, but that "psal lecha" — the inferior (stone-dust) is for you. Indeed, our Sages taught that Moses grew wealthy from the sapphire stone-dust that fell away during the carving.[8]

The hidden message here is that material wealth is "psal," inferior bits of dust. There is no reason to grow arrogant on account of having collected a great deal of inferior bits of dust. Regardless of the financial value, compared

---

[5] *Exodus* 32:18.

[6] Divrei Yisrael al Hatorah.

[7] *Exodus* 34:1.

[8] See Rashi on *Exodus* 34:21. Tanchuma on *Shemot* 29 and *Vayikra Rabbah* 32:2.

to the Torah and things spiritual, they are *"psal,"* small and inferior.[9] Even those who are blessed with wealth, as Moses was, must remember, as Moses did, that all wealth comes from G-d.

Because G-d is the Source of our blessing, our humble gratitude belongs to Him Alone.

---

[9] Divrei Yisrael al Hatorah.

"But it seems to me that trust in G-d entails surrender. Surrender really goes against the grain for me; maybe it goes against human nature..."

FORWARD VISION

HAIR-RAISING DRIVE

A friend of mine and his father were driving in the dead of night on a treacherous mountain road with razor-sharp curves and sheer cliff drops. His father drove along nonchalantly, seemingly oblivious to the danger. When he asked his father how he could be so nonchalant, his father replied, "My diabetes has damaged my peripheral vision."

Simply put, his father could see only what was in front of them — and in front of them, the road was clear. That the narrow road dropped precipitously into dangerous ravines did not perturb him. He couldn't see the drops and took no notice of them. What he couldn't see didn't worry him.

EMBRACING THE PRESENT

What a lesson for life. Our concern with what could have been or what might yet be distracts us from what is. How many people live for their vacations? Their days at work pass by with agonizing slowness, intended only as a prelude to the next vacation. With their minds focused on last year's memories and next year's plans, how can they notice this year's blessings?

When our ancestors stood before Mount Sinai, G-d asked them if they would accept his Torah. They answered, "We will do and we will listen!" They pledged to obey G-d's commandments first and ask questions later. They'd had years of exposure in Egypt to the other available paths. Once they saw the salvations of G-d, they embraced Judaism and stopped questioning. They stopped looking back.

How did they know they had made the right decision? They jumped in with perfect faith in G-d, and once they chose to jump in, they were committed. If they would question everything G-d told them, they wouldn't be free to travel the path they had chosen. They would always be distracted by looking elsewhere.

The time for deliberation is before we make our decision. Once the decision is made, it's time to let it play out. Silencing our questions, at that point, allows us to discover how our choice resonates with us, to come to feel at home with it, to grow in it, and then to be thankful that we gave ourselves the chance.[1]

SEEKING DISCOUNTS

I don't enjoy shopping. I prefer to find what I need and leave the store. I know that not everyone shops that way. Many people like to compare prices in all their neighborhood stores and ensure that they receive the best possible deal. I often wonder if it's worth the effort. They may end up paying less than I do, but, unaware of what I'm missing, I'm content with what I have. I have friends who stay up all night to research the best possible deal for an airline ticket. After making their purchase, they live in dread of having missed a better deal. If they discover that a seatmate on the plane paid less for his or her ticket, they're inconsolable, unable to enjoy the flight.

Is it really important to seek out information that can no longer be of help to us? We're already on the road. Why do we need to know how steep the drop is? We've already made our purchase. Why do we need to know how much someone else paid? We're already Jews. Why do we need to know what other religions teach?

Many argue that it's important to keep an open mind. It *is* important, but as a rabbi I know often quips, "If you open your mind too much, your brain might fall out." If you constantly seek out whatever kernels of truth there

---

[1] Our ancestors never pledged to not question at all. They pledged only to obey the laws of the Torah first and ask questions later. They promised to observe each commandment out of obedience, and then seek out its inner meaning and reasons. The idea here is that we must deliberate before we make our choice, but once the choice is made, we must give our chosen path a chance to resonate. If we question every move and scrutinize every detail after we commit to it, the end result will always be a lack of commitment.

may be in the paths you didn't choose, you will neglect the countless sheaves of truth in the path you did choose.

EXPOSURE OR IMMERSION

I remember a discussion I had with a Jewish man whose daughter adopted a non-Jewish child and had him converted to Judaism.

Conversions of children before the age of bar or bat mitzvah are provisional. The child, on reaching the religious age of maturity, decides whether to endorse the conversion or reject it. To make an informed decision, the child must be educated in the ways of Torah. So the *beit din* (Jewish court) insisted that the child be placed in a Jewish day school.

The grandfather of the adopted child argued that the *beit din*'s insistence would prejudice the child toward Judaism. "How can my grandson choose freely, when he will be exposed only to the Jewish path?!" he demanded. "He ought to be exposed to both paths so he will understand what he is rejecting."

I answered that it doesn't require training to discover the pleasures that await on the streets. That can be learned in a day or even an hour. Jewish children are keenly aware that their mothers don't shop in the non-kosher section of the supermarket and that their friends don't go to the mall or theater on Shabbat. They are sufficiently exposed to secular culture to know what they're missing. However, to understand that these sacrifices are privileges rather than burdens *does* require training. The only way to get a sense of the meaning, sanctity, and Divine fulfillment that Judaism offers is to immerse oneself in the experience. Mere exposure is not sufficient. One cannot know the serenity of Shabbat without having experienced it. To experience it truly and deeply, one has to observe consecutive Shabbats. Occasional Shabbat observance doesn't convey the inner contentment that comes from deep conviction of and from commitment to the sanctity of the day. When Shabbat is observed occasionally, it feels more like a vacation than a Shabbat. The same holds true for all the tenets and practices of our faith.

I told the grandfather that his grandson's choice will be free only if it is informed. If the child is denied an opportunity to immerse himself in Judaism, he will never know the beauty of Judaism. But if the child is denied an opportunity to immerse himself in secularism, he will still discover its attraction.

IN THE DESERT

This may be the reason G-d instructed our ancestors to remain in the desert for forty years, after they received the Torah. Free from confusing distraction, they were provided an opportunity to be immersed fully in the Torah and its way of life.

This may also be why our Sages ordained that the Torah portion of *Bamidbar*, translated as "In the Desert," should be chanted every year on the Shabbat before the holiday of Shavuot, the day the Torah was given to our People. It is a reminder that grasping the soul of Torah requires immersion. We must silence the chatter of our minds and banish all distracting thought. We must explore the Torah with single-minded devotion, as we focus our attention on the Divine.

Yes, trust does entail surrender. We surrender our ego, and even some of our independence. Judaism — and life — cannot be fully embraced without at least a modicum of trust. But we can learn that such surrender is in our best interest.

"In general, I don't have a problem trusting G-d. But how can I trust Him on the question of why people suffer?"

FAITH AND SUFFERING
A MOTHER'S PAIN
A mother who was concluding the seven days of mourning, after her child's death went to see her Rebbe. Through her tears, she begged him to tell her why it had been decreed that her beloved child had to die.

The Rebbe asked, "Do you really want to know?"

"Yes, of course I do," she said.

"Are you sure?" asked the Rebbe.

We all want to know the unknowable secrets of G-d's mysterious ways. As we cry, our tears mingle with the tears of generations; our cry is the echo of millennia: "Why do the righteous suffer? Why do the innocent die?" G-d is Just, and would never allow suffering without cause; of that we are certain. But what is the cause that could justify such suffering?

Do we really want to know? Will such knowledge help us? "Yes," we reply. "It will bring closure, and allow us to make peace with our suffering." But perhaps if we listen to our own words, we will realize how wrong we are. Is suffering something with which we really want to make peace? Is it not comforting to know that our suffering is somehow connected to an Infinite, cosmic plan? Do we want to reduce our pain to proportions that neatly fit the tiny confines of our human mind?

THE BURNING BUSH
Moses was once given an opportunity to understand the reason for human suffering. He was herding a flock of sheep, when he came upon a Burning Bush. Flames licked the twigs of the thorn bush, but the bush was not consumed.[1] Biblical commentary teaches that this spectacle was symbolic. The

---

[1] *Exodus* 3:1–6.

bush represents man; the thorns represent human suffering. In the flames, Moses saw the pain that ripples through us when we are stricken and in grief. Moses was intrigued. The flames did not consume the bush. Pain does not consume the person. Why not?[2]

As Moses stood and pondered, G-d offered to teach him the reason behind human suffering. G-d offered to show him the great benefits derived from suffering, the blessings that grow out of affliction, the strength that springs forth from pain. Moses, having witnessed the pain of his brethren in Egypt, was naturally curious. He came forward.

Before he could approach, he was informed that he was about to enter a holy place. "Take off your shoes," said a Heavenly voice. "You stand on holy ground." In the presence of another's suffering, we must tread softly, because the ground of suffering is hallowed. The time of grief is not a time for words. We don't talk. We don't explain. We simply hold hands. We offer empathy and silent support.[3]

CHANGE OF HEART

Moses removed his shoes and approached ... But at this point the narrative takes a sharp and unexpected turn. Moses, who had been so eager to approach, so eager to learn, suddenly demurred. He turned away and was afraid to look at G-d. What happened here? Why did Moses suddenly change his mind?

Moses stood poised to discover the true reason for human suffering and that, according to one commentary, is why he shied away.[4] Moses was a man who burned with a sense of moral justice. When he saw the innocent suffer, he wanted to know why. But then, when he was about to be told why, he real-

---

[2] *Shemos Rabbah* 2:5. See also Rashi's commentary on the Burning Bush.

[3] I heard this explanation from my colleague and friend Rabbi Yossi Jacobsob.

[4] See Covenant and Conversation, 5768, *Shemot*, Of What was Moses Afraid, by Rabbi Lord Jonathan Sacks. Available at www.chiefrabbi.org

ized that he really didn't want to know.[5] Moses feared that if he truly understood the reason for human suffering, he would never be able to empathize with those in pain. If he truly understood the benefit of grief, he would be immune to the cries of a mourning mother. How could he comfort his People, if he could not feel their pain?

THE PAIN THAT WE WELCOME

Imagine standing in line at an airport security booth before boarding your plane. The line is moving very slowly. Worried about missing your flight, you inquire about the delay and learn that security personnel have paused for a union-mandated coffee break.

Now imagine standing in the same line and discovering that progress has stalled because security precautions required a more thorough inspection of a particular bag. The same amount of time has elapsed, your line has stalled in both cases. Yet in the first case, you feel consternation. And in the second, you feel relief. Because when we are aware of the benefits, we are prepared to accept the delay.

The same is true of pain. There are many forms of pain. There is pain of illness and there is pain of recovery. They are both painful but they are not equal. Illness is a scourge and we do all we can to escape it. Recovery is a blessing and we do all we can to welcome it. It is no less painful, but, aware of its benefits, we welcome it.

BETTER NOT TO KNOW

Imagine a mother approaching Moses for solace after burying her child. If he had accepted G-d's offer and now understood the cosmic benefits that precipitated the child's demise, could Moses have truly empathized with her pain? What if he tried to comfort the mother by explaining the reasons for her child's demise? Can you imagine her horror at hearing her child's death explained away like a delay in an airport security line? "Thank you, G-d," said Moses. "But I decline." Much as he longed to know the truth, Moses felt

---

[5] *Shemot* Rabbah 2:6.

that he could not afford to learn an answer that would cost him a portion of his humanity, even as it offered him a glimpse of Divinity. That was not a price he was prepared to pay, not if he was expected to shepherd the human flock that awaited him.[6]

We, too, burn with a sense of justice as we demand to know the reasons behind our tragedies. We must ask ourselves the question that the Rebbe asked the grieving mother. Do we really want to know?[7]

The truest form of knowledge is the knowledge that we do not know.

---

[6] Later in the narrative, G-d told Moses to tell the Jewish People that He will always be with them in their times of suffering (*Exodus* 3:14. See also *Shemot Rabbah* 3:6.). Moses refused to understand the reason behind human suffering, so G-d told him to simply accept that there is a reason, but that this reason transcends human understanding. G-d is with us when we suffer and He suffers right alongside us. This is true despite our lack of understanding about why G-d chooses to make us suffer.

[7] A curious aspect of human nature is that we often demand an answer to the question of why — but when the answer is offered, it seldom satisfies us. On the contrary, it irritates. The reason is simple. The pain is greater than the logical response. When we are offered a logical response, we instinctively feel that it does not address the source of our pain. Overwhelming pain cannot be reduced to logical propositions.

"Sometimes I get so discouraged and melancholy. How can I find the strength to go on during such times?

THE NIGHT BELONGS TO JACOB

THREE PRAYERS — WHY?

The Patriarchs — Abraham, Isaac, and Jacob — are not only symbols of our past. Giant figures in our long history, they are our spiritual guides, whose character and perseverance model and set the tone for their descendants and continue to have an impact on Jewish practice to this day.

One notable area in which this is true is in our three daily prayer services, which were, in fact, instituted by them.[1] Abraham instituted the morning service, Isaac the afternoon service, and Jacob the evening service. Though each Patriarch was complete in his entire spiritual and moral repertoire, each exbodied a particular virtue, which was his essence, and also his contribution to us. Each of the three services reflects the character of its respective author.[2]

A day consists of morning, afternoon, and evening. Each stage in the day has a distinct quality, presents a distinct challenge, and offers a unique opportunity. Thus, the prayers assigned to each stage of the day elicit the specific Divine energies appropriate for the particular challenges of that time.

THREE STAGES

The first stage begins at dawn, a time filled with promise and potential, as we anticipate the new day that lies ahead. The prevailing Divine energy during this time is one of hope and optimism. Fittingly, Abraham, a man of positive spirit and infinite optimism, instituted *Shacharit*, the morning prayer.

As the day proceeds and we engage in its many difficult tasks, however rewarding, the morning's enthusiasm wanes. Through the afternoon, we face our challenges one at a time, intent on achieving our goals by the end of the

---

[1] *Babylonian Talmud; Brachot* 26b.

[2] For more detail, see Derech Hashem, Pirkei Tefillah.

day. But the day is long and, if we are to succeed, we must unflaggingly maintain our resolve. The prevailing energy during this time is one of determination. Fittingly, Isaac, especially known for his firm resolve, instituted *Minchah*, the afternoon prayer.

As the end of the day draws near, we tire. Darkness encroaches and the mood grows melancholy. We see that daylight and warmth do not last forever; we sense our own mortality. Looking back at the day, we cannot escape the awareness of how much was left unaccomplished, how very much yet remains to be done. The morning's energy and enthusiasm and the afternoon's disciplined resolve have faded. Night envelops us in a cloak of uncertainty. Can we overcome the chill of night and seek refuge in G-d's warmth? Jacob knew that we could, and accordingly instituted *Maariv*, the evening prayer.

And who better to instill in us this conviction than Jacob? His life was a string of dark moments, difficult trials, and overwhelming challenges. Yet he never despaired. When all that he had hoped and worked for appeared unattainable, he remained committed. In his most bitter, heartbreaking, and tragic moments, his trust never wavered.

HEAVY-FOOTED BUT LIGHTHEARTED

Forced to flee from his family and wander to a strange and foreign land[3] Jacob knew that he might never see his home again.[4] As he set out to create a new life for himself, he should have had a heavy heart. Alone in the dark, as the first day came to an end, he had good reason to be afraid. Instead, he turned a situation of despair into a moment of inspiration, a moment that left its mark for all generations.

As the sun set on that first day of his journey, the Torah tells us, "*Vayifga bamakom*"[5] he "encountered the place," the exact place where his descendants

---

[3] *Genesis* 27.

[4] See the commentary of *Kli Yakar* on *Genesis* 28:10.

[5] *Genesis* 28.

would build the future Temple. What did Jacob do there? Our Sages relate that he established the evening service.

As darkness descended, and with his future path uncertain, what was it that inspired him to establish this prayer service? The answer lies in the Torah's words: *"Vayifga bamakom, ki ba hashemesh."* These words are usually translated as "he encountered the place, as the sun set." However, a literal translation yields a different meaning: "he encountered the inside of the place, because the sun set." In other words, the occurrence of the sunset, at the precise moment he reached the Temple Mount, revealed to him the inner purpose of the place.

What did the sunset convey to him?

LIGHT WITHIN DARKNESS

The light that filled the Temple was not a physical light but a transcendent light, reserved for that holy place.[6] This was the light that Jacob encountered when he approached the Mount. At the same time, he noticed that the sun had set — though it was still midday. The physical light had departed, replaced by the spiritual light.

An ordinary person would not have made the connection. But Jacob did. He understood the meaning of this juxtaposition — outshone by the light of the Temple, the ordinary light had given way.[7] The darkness he was experiencing, the absence of physical light, was not due to nightfall; it was too early for night. The physical darkness was due to the presence of a much greater light, a quality of light too powerful for the eye to detect.

An ordinary person would have experienced only the darkness. But Jacob "encountered" — detected — the *"inside"* of the darkness; he knew its deeper

---

[6] See Sefat Emet 5648.

[7] The windows in the Temple were narrow on the inside and wide on the outside, because they were not intended to illuminate the Temple with the light from the outside but to illuminate the world with the light of the Temple. See *Bamidbar Rabbah* 15:2.

meaning. He understood that this darkness was shrouded in a rarefied light so G-dly as to lie beyond the perception of the human eye. Night enveloped Jacob, but he saw only light. Rather than chilling melancholy, Jacob was overcome by inspiration and joy.

This unique vision, made possible by the darkness, inspired him to establish a prayer of gratitude for the gift called night.[8] Jacob pierced the veil of darkness and its underlying despair. And, through this prayer, he shared his profound vision with us. He saw that night is not the end of today — but the beginning of tomorrow. Indeed, it is only the rest and relaxation of the night that refreshes us and enables us to face the light of morning.[9]

With this evening prayer, Jacob enabled us to draw Divine energy into the wearying and demoralizing night. With this prayer, we prevent the night from shattering our glorious dream. With this prayer, we anticipate tomorrow's dawn. Because this prayer gives us the courage to face tonight's darkness.[10]

---

[8] We thank G-d every morning for "forming light and creating darkness." Should we not first thank G-d for the darkness, and then for the light that redeems us from the dark? The darkness that we are thankful for is of the kind that conceals an even greater light. Since that light is beyond human perception, we are incapable of seeing it; it appears to us simply as darkness. For more details on the supernal nature of darkness, see Torat Chayim p. 60.

[9] He prayed at that moment as he had never prayed before. The Torah tells us that he collected the stones from the ground around him. Kabbalah teaches that stones are like letters. Just as stones build walls and homes, so do letters build words and sentences. Indeed, G-d used letters and words to create the world. Chassidic thought explains that Jacob used the letters through which G-d created that particular moment and rearranged them to form the words of his prayer. In other words, he used the very darkness that would have frightened an ordinary person to create a prayer of inspiration, strength, and hope. For more detail, see Torah Ohr, *parshat Vayeitzei*, and Sefat Emet, parshat *Vayetzei*.

[10] See Sefat Emet 5648, that the three Temples also closely resemble the three stages of our day. The First Temple, like the morning, was filled with promise

Our Patriarch Jacob teaches us that even the darkest night can be brighter, warmer, and more inspiring than day. When we pray the evening prayer, we thank G-d for Jacob, without whom we might not have survived our long and bitter nights.

---

and infinite potential; it was permeated by the love of G-d for the Jewish People. The Second Temple was permeated by a sense of duty. It stood during a trying time for the Jewish nation, a time filled with challenges and difficulties — like the afternoon. Through it all, we did our best to triumph. The Third Temple, which we pray will soon be built, will remain eternal. It will never be followed by another exile; its light will not be countered by darkness. From where will it receive this strength? From Jacob, the Patriarch of truth. Just as truth can never be compromised, so did Jacob's commitment never waver. The dark could not unsettle him, as the Exile cannot unsettle the Third Temple. Jacob's travels brought him to the Temple Mount; our wanderings will carry us there, too. When we arrive, we will discover that the essence of the Exile is, like the night, a light of unprecedented intensity.

PART THREE – HUMILITY, UNITY AND LOVE

"It's inspiring to learn about the Patriarchs, Moses and Aaron. And I know that every generation has its 'Moses' and 'Aaron,' too, who can help them grow. But I feel bad that I'm not like them, that I'm just an ordinary Jew."

THE SILENT FLAME
HARDLY ANY SPLASH AT ALL

One of the criteria by which professional high divers are rated is the angle in which they enter the water and the resultant splash factor. Entering the water at a twisted angle increases the splash factor. Entering the water at a vertical angle minimizes the splash factor. The smaller the splash factor, the higher the rating the diver receives.

Judaism is no different. There are dynamic, spirited Jews who worship with great fervor, who really "make a big splash," and there are simple, unnoticed, but dependable Jews who worship with quiet commitment. Both are important. The spirited Jew provides leadership and inspires the masses. The simple Jew is always there, always committed, regardless of circumstance. In the eyes of man, the former generates more attention. In the eyes of G-d the latter is at least as important. G-d loves the spirited Jews for their influence and flair. G-d loves the simple Jews for their firm and permanent commitment, their purity of service for Him Alone.

A CRESTFALLEN AARON

This story takes us back to the final day of the Altar's inaugural ceremony. Each of the tribal princes had brought an offering. As evidenced by the celestial flames that consumed them, the offerings were accepted on High. The public nature of the offerings, and the celestial flames they summoned from the skies, inspired the masses. Their souls aflame with love; they put the Golden Calf behind them. Their hearts overflowing with gratitude, they dedicated themselves to G-d. Their spirits brimming with enthusiasm, they were wholly and purely inspired to serve.

Aaron felt dejected.[1] As the High Priest, he was chiefly responsible for the sacrificial rite and should have been at the center of the inaugural activity. Yet he was not given a role. It was not his personal glory that worried him, but the destiny of the nation. Nine months earlier, he had unwittingly led the nation to the Golden Calf. Now that he was seemingly rebuffed by G-d, he worried that he, and by extension the People, was not fully forgiven.

G-D RESPONDS

Aaron's sentiments were apparent on High, and G-d responded with consoling words. "Fear not, Aaron. You were not invited to inaugurate the Altar, because your role is greater than the service of the Altar. You shall kindle the lights of the holy Menorah."

At first glance, G-d's response seems curious. Why do the lights of the Menorah transcend the celestial flames stimulated by the offerings? One might further ask, Why did G-d not console Aaron with the incense offering, which surely transcended the inaugural offerings? The incense was offered on a golden altar that stood in the inner sanctum, while the inaugural offerings were placed on a copper altar that stood in the courtyard. G-d could also have consoled Aaron with the promise of the service on Yom Kippur. Aaron, as High Priest, was permitted to enter the Inner Sanctuary, the most sacred chamber in the Temple, on this most sacred day. This service surely transcended that of the inaugural offerings. Why did this service not constitute sufficient consolation for Aaron?

THE POWER OF A FLAME

A flame produces light and warmth. But that is not its only strength. The flame's secret is that it overcomes the deepest and greatest darkness. No matter how deep the darkness, it recedes before a flame. No matter how deep the gloom, the flame soothes, comforts, and illuminates. The flame is small and unassuming, but in its glow everything is softened. Sharp edges of difficulties are blunted; faith and hope are quietly restored.

---

[1] *Numbers* 5:2. See Rashi, ibid.

One of the flame's most profound features is the way that it gives of itself to serve others. A flame gives of itself and is not diminished in the process. One flame ignites a thousand others, and remains as powerful and as illuminating as before. This is the secret of its ability to stand up to and conquer the darkness of night.[2]

THE ENDURING FLAME

This is why the flames burned miraculously for eight days and nights during Chanukah, even while the Altar lay in disrepair. This is also why the Chanukah lights continue to glow long after the Temple was destroyed. The Altar is destroyed, the sacrificial rites have long ceased, and the bitter darkness of Exile has descended, yet those original lights of the Temple's Menorah continue to illuminate, through our Shabbat and Chanukah candles.[3] Indeed, it is the nature of light that it never succumbs to darkness. Light does not recede when darkness encroaches; on the contrary, that is when its mission begins.

This is why Aaron's inaugural calling surpassed that of the tribal princes. Beautiful and inspiring as their offerings were, they were only as enduring as the Altar itself. Aaron was invited to kindle a light that would burn long after the Temple would be destroyed and the darkness of night would descend. His flame would outlast even its own Menorah.

---

[2] The one force that a flame cannot overcome is apathy. The apathetic will watch the flame burn off its fuel and not rush to refill it. A flame that is permitted to burn out cannot be brought back to life. A new flame will have to take its place.

[3] Nachmanides on *Numbers* 5:2. Not only were the Chanukah lights kindled before the Altar was restored, they burned in a Temple where the Altar itself was unable to summon celestial flames. The *Babylonian Talmud* (*Yoma* 21b) explains that five principal elements that existed in the First Temple were notably missing in the Second Temple. One of them was the celestial flame that consumed the sacrifices. It was during the Second Temple Era that the Chanukah miracle occurred. See also Kli Yakar on *Numbers* 5:2.

THE SIMPLE JEW

Simple, quiet Jews worship G-d in the same way that candles radiate light, intent only on fulfilling their purpose. Humble and unassuming, they serve out of obedience. They are not suffused with ecstasy or filled with bliss. They do not tremble in awe or exult in enthusiasm. They are not aglow with joy or aflame with love. They simply are. They serve G-d because G-d wants to be served.[4]

This kind of service is long lasting. Long after love has waned and awe has dissipated, long after the ecstasy has calmed and the joy has quieted, these Jews will continue to serve. These Jews will be in a position to rekindle the spiritual light of those, whose enthusiasm has waned. [5]

Such can be the power of our own contribution, the quiet contribution of the the ordinary simple Jew — even Aaron aspired to it.

---

[4] Noam Elimelech, ibid.

[5] See also Likutei Sichot XXXVIII, p. 38.

"I still can't seem to get away from making comparisons. And everybody else seems to come out looking better ... "

IN THE TRENCHES
THE PAWN
What is your favorite piece on the chessboard? The queen, knight, castle, and bishop are all important, but the pawn has one capacity that the others don't — "promotion." The pawn is not at all versatile; it inches forward one step at a time. Yet when it reaches the other side, it can be "promoted," transformed into any chess-piece that the player chooses. It can even become a queen.

Angels are holier than humans. They are passionate about G-d, ecstatic in worship, and thrilled to bask in the Divine Presence. Their melodies reverberate through the heavens, and their prayers make the hosts of heaven tremble. Yet they are forever chained to their original state. They cannot upgrade to a higher level. They cannot improve. They cannot grow.

G-D'S SANCTUARY
G-d promised Moses, "Make a Sanctuary for Me and I will dwell in it. "This promise applies not only to sanctuaries of mortar, brick, silver, and gold, but also to sanctuaries of heart and soul. G-d promised to dwell in the hearts of those who transform their lives into sanctuaries for Him.[1]

Some Jews live exalted, spiritual, holy, lives. They are altruistic, righteous, and devout, great Torah scholars, fervently committed to *mitzvot* and enraptured with love for G-d. Such Jews certainly turn their lives into sanctuaries for G-d. But what of the rest of us? What of ordinary Jews like you and me? We struggle every day against our inclinations. We are beset by jealousies and rage, phobias and fears, weaknesses and pride. Every day, we struggle to overcome our human vicissitudes. Sometimes we succeed; sometimes we don't. Can we also become sanctuaries for G-d? Can our existence also be holy?

---

[1] *Exodus* 25:8.

G-d's answer is yes. G-d's Temple is built one brick at a time. His sanctuary within our hearts is built one struggle at a time. Unlike the other pieces on the chessboard, we cannot take mighty leaps or undertake fancy maneuvers. Much like the pawn, we crawl forward one step at a time. But with each step, we draw closer to the ideal. With each step, we are transformed into miniature sanctuaries for G-d. Every time we overcome our base natures and do something for G-d, we add a brick to His Sanctuary. Every struggle is holy. Notwithstanding tomorrow's struggle, today's triumph is an eternal brick in G-d's magnificent Sanctuary.

THE Infantry

Let's consider a military analogy. An army must have many weapons in its arsenal. Tanks, planes, artillery, are all important. But they are not enough. To conquer the enemy, an army needs foot soldiers, an infantry.

The general, who plans the overall strategy, makes a crucial contribution to the war effort. The admiral, who directs the navy, makes a similar contribution. Fighters and bombers destroy large swathes of the enemy's infrastructure. Long-range guns and artillery create large gaps in the enemy lines. An army cannot progress without these formidable weapons. But these weapons are not enough. To win the war, foot soldiers must be placed on the battle field.

The infantry fights in the trenches. They subdue one enemy at a time. They conquer one inch of territory at a time. Bombers and tanks wreak havoc, but the infantry wins the war. Their fight is not always pretty and they don't win every skirmish. Comrades are often lost to injury or even death. They falter and stumble, they are sullied and dirtied, but they engage the enemy directly. They bring triumph to the cause and victory to the country.

This analogy can be applied to our discussion. The great *tzaddikim* and the famous scholars are Judaism's "big guns." They do wonders for G-d's Sanctuary; they lay the foundation and establish the infrastructure. But they cannot build the Sanctuary. To build the Sanctuary, bricks are needed. And bricks are shaped by the hard work of foot soldiers. Every time we overcome our ego, rein in our temper or control our cravings, we lay a brick in G-d's

Sanctuary. The righteous cannot control their cravings, because they never crave. Only the foot soldiers can shape and lay G-d's holy bricks.

Like the pawn, our struggle may seem inconsequential in the greater scheme, but our growth and resulting contribution, are vital. We, the foot soldiers, through our slow, but steady growth, through our limited, but inexorable transformation, build G-d's eternal Sanctuary.

THE UNDERDOG

In a way, G-d loves the daily struggle of the ordinary Jew more than the great achievements of the extraordinary Jew.

A talking bird attracts attention, a talking human does not. Why is that? Because human interest is stimulated by the remarkable and unexpected triumph of those who have invested extraordinary effort. For example, in professional sports, when the better team wins, they are given short shrift. We were expecting them to win, and without much effort. But when the underdogs win, they're cheered for weeks. We know how much harder they had to try. The expected is not interesting. Only the unexpected sparks our interest.

A cardinal principle in Jewish theology is that much about G-d can be inferred from the study of human nature. As Job wrote, "From my flesh, I perceive the Lord."[2] The Chassidic masters taught that this particular aspect of human nature is highly instructive. The reason we appreciate accomplishments that entail great effort is because G-d does.[3] The angels pray to G-d; they worship and are completely devoted. But G-d expects that from them; there's no effort involved. The righteous are also highly devout in prayer and worship. But G-d expects it from them, too. This is not to say that G-d doesn't love their devotion, just that the joy He derives from it is limited.

---

[2] Job 19:26.
[3] Torah Ohr 21b.

We ordinary Jews, conceited and proud, self-centered and shortsighted, narcissistic and arrogant, command G-d's attention. We are the underdogs, from whom not much can reasonably be expected. But when we succeed, when we exchange apathy for enthusiasm and hesitation for determination, G-d is, as it were, enthralled. Every tiniest struggle draws Divine attention. Every victory stimulates Divine joy. Every deed is important. [4]

Not everyone was meant to be a scholar. Some Jews — you and I — were meant to be simple bricklayers. But we, the bricklayers, will build G-d's eternal home.

---

[4] This essay is based on Sefer Mamaarim 1950, p. 111.

"But ... I still keep feeling that I want to do something really great. I mean, isn't that what we're created for?"

LOYAL TO WHOM?

THE VICE PRESIDENT

After twenty years with the company, the senior vice president was invited to the president's office. "We have been experiencing a rash of theft in the mail room," said the president. "We suspect the mail room supervisor. This position must be filled by someone we can trust. You have demonstrated loyalty to the company for more than two decades, and we have decided to appoint you to this position."

The vice president was incensed. "For twenty years, I have devoted my energies to your company!" he objected. "And now you demote me to the mail room?"

As he stormed out of the office, he heard the president mutter, "You were loyal to a fault. But only to your position — never to the company."

Indeed, it is possible to devote a lifetime to enhance the company for which we work, the social circle to which we belong, or the marriage to which we are pledged, and yet be committed only to ourselves.

THE UNREACHABLE REWARD

When Moses led our ancestors through the desert, they were promised a wonderful reward at the end of their journey: a Land flowing with milk and honey. Anxious about the future that awaited them in the Land of Israel, our ancestors sent a delegation of spies to scout the Land. On their return, the spies reported that it was an amazing land, blessed with gargantuan fruit, towering mountains, lush valleys, and plentiful streams. Its inhabitants seemed healthy and strong and its economy thriving and prosperous. Its borders were secured by fearsome warriors, powerful armies, and naturally secure perimeters.

So what was wrong? Why did the nation greet this report with tears?

They were afraid of the fearsome armies and the naturally secure borders. They envisioned defeat and massacre on the battlefields, and tearfully bemoaned their fate. This literal reading of our ancestors' reluctance to push forth and claim their Promised Land justifies the Divine response. Through Moses, G-d rebuked the people for their lack of faith and punished ten of the twelve spies.[1]

AN IDYLLIC LIFE

The Mystics, however, share with us another perspective, from which our ancestors emerge in a more positive light. As they see it, the spies are seen not as unfaithful heretics, but as devoted saints who could not stand to surrender their holy way of life.

In the desert, our ancestors lived an idyllic life. They were not distracted by economic burdens or social entanglements and they had no worldly worries or mundane concerns; their every need was bountifully provided by G-d. Bread fell daily from Heaven and water gushed forth from a miraculous rock. Garments grew with their bodies and were laundered daily by the Clouds of Glory. The Clouds protected them from the desert elements, leaving them with nothing to worry about. Their sole occupation was the study of Torah. They came to know, fear, and love G-d. They lived a life of purpose and devotion, in a pious and peaceful environment. Every day was a new frontier in the uncharted paths of spiritual pursuit.

SOON TO BE SHATTERED

With such an idyllic existence, they were apprehensive about the future. When they contemplated the Promised Land, they experienced a hint of trepidation. Could they possibly preserve this otherworldly existence in their Promised Land? They would have to conquer the Land, divide the tribal lots, and apportion them. They would have to raise an army, wage wars, establish judicial systems, collect taxes, and organize the infrastructure of government. They would have to cultivate fields, harvest crops, and feed their families. Would they find time for devotion and meditation?

---

[1] *Numbers* 13–14.

They sent spies to confirm their suspicions, and were met with a sobering report. "Yes," reported the spies. "The Land overflows with material blessing." They *would* need to farm the luscious lands, fish the plentiful rivers, hike the towering mountains, and inhabit the deep valleys. They *would* need to defend their borders and raise an army. They *would not* be free to devote themselves to Torah and to spirituality.

At this the nation balked. "No!" they cried. "We don't want that kind of life. We're accustomed to our life of ascetic holiness, and have no desire for such a Promised Land. We would rather forfeit the Land if, in return, we might be permitted to serve G-d in peace."

SOLDIERS IN G-D'S ARMY

Admirable though their desire was, it was wrong. Judaism is not about realizing personal goals; it is about fulfilling G-d's goals. It is not about enhancing our prestige; it is about being a good servant. The Torah does not strive to create spiritually minded ascetics; it strives to create Jews who are obedient to G-d's Will.

Our loyalty mustn't be to our position within the company, but to the company itself. We should be ready to serve Him wherever and however He wants us to serve. If the boss wants us in the mail room, we don't belong in the front office. We each have our position and we should be honored to accept it. If G-d wanted our ancestors in the Land of Israel, then they belonged in the Land of Israel, even if they felt that it was better for them in the desert. When G-d commands, we must obey and follow.[2]

We were not created to achieve great things. We were created to serve G-d. G-d doesn't seek a spectacular achiever but a loyal servant. As our ancestors learned, it is only through serving G-d that great things can be achieved. After all, we are soldiers in His army.

---

[2] Likutei Torah, *Bamidbar* 36b.

"If the primary point of Judaism is to serve G-d, how is it different from other faiths? Don't all religions speak of serving G-d"

WHAT IS JUDAISM?

UNIQUE

What makes Judaism unique? Some call it the religion of ethics. Others point to Judaism's spirit of open dialogue. Yet others invoke Judaism's ancient tradition. These answers do not suffice. Judaism is ethical, but so are many other religions. Judaism encourages open dialogue, but so do many other movements. Judaism is an ancient religion, but there are other ancient religions. What does Judaism offer that no other religion does?

The answer can be summed up in two words: Mount Sinai. Judaism is the only religion that was established with a direct transmission from G-d to the masses. All other religions originated with a prophecy, and are thus predicated on the integrity of a single prophet. Adherents must decide for themselves whether they trust the prophet and accept the prophecy; their faith is a product of personal conviction. Judaism originated at Sinai, where the entire Jewish nation witnessed the appearance of G-d, and received the Ten Commandments. They did not need to rely on the integrity of Moses and his prophecy; they saw G-d for themselves; they shared in the prophecy and *knew* that the commandments were truly Divine. Our religion was not born of personal conviction; it was born in response to Divine commandment. A Jew is thus one who follows G-d not out of personal conviction, but out of obedience.[1]

---

[1] That Jews witnessed G-d at Sinai and received the Ten Commandments is an article of faith. Yet it is possible to argue that it is more rational to suppose that this event did occur than to suggest that it did not. Throughout the world, there are millions of people who learned about the Sinai encounter from their parents. These parents heard about it from *their* parents, who in turn heard about it from *their* parents. This chain of tradition goes back thousands of years, but it had to originate somewhere. Is it reasonable to suppose that at some point in history, a group of scholars convinced an entire generation that G-d had appeared to their

AN ACCOMPLISHED MAN

Abraham was a great philosopher. When he was three years old, he carefully examined every faith system, finally embracing monotheism. As a young boy, he was renowned for his sterling character. As an adult, he gained fame for his morality, generosity, and hospitality. He was loved for his kindness and respected for his conviction. A trailblazer in the philosophy of religion, he was a scholar of original, even revolutionary, thought, who converted thousands to his way of thinking. Powerful monarchs persecuted him for his faith, and even sentenced him to death. But miraculously, Abraham escaped execution.[2]

The fascinating tales about Abraham are preserved in the annals of Jewish tradition, but the Torah itself is strangely silent on this era of Abraham's life. Abraham is introduced in the Torah at the ripe old age of seventy-five. That

---

ancestors at Sinai? Is it not reasonable to assume that at least some people would have rejected this as a fantasy? Yet not a single objection of this nature has ever been recorded. This is especially astounding in light of the fact that Jews are a contentious people, who never have shied away from public dispute. The Talmud is replete with scholarly dispute. Following the Talmudic model, the integrity of the Sinai encounter should have been greeted with skepticism and treated to a full and public debate.

Some have suggested that Moses concocted the entire Sinai story and convinced his coreligionists that they were there. To such people, I suggest the following exercise: Try to convince your friend that you visited the North Pole. Can you convince him? Depending on your ability as a storyteller, you might convince him. Now try to convince your friend that *he* visited the North Pole with you, though he has no memory of this. It stretches the bounds of credulity to suppose that you might convince him. Is it any more reasonable to suppose that Moses convinced his *entire* generation that they experienced the Sinai encounter, if they had no memory of it? By contrast, is it any less reasonable to suppose that the original transmitters of this tradition believed it because they experienced it themselves? For more information, see Shaarei Emunah 52.

[2] Recorded in many Midrashic sources, including *Bereshit* Rabbah and *Pirkei D'Rebbi Eliezer*.

was when G-d directed him to leave his homeland, where he had achieved so much, and to travel to an undisclosed destination.[3]

FATHER OF JUDAISM

It is not because of his great achievements or the fine qualities that he displayed during the first seventy-five years of his life that Abraham is deemed our first Patriarch. These were important qualities for the father of Judaism to possess, but they did not define his Jewishness.

Abraham became a Jew when he experienced that which is unique to Judaism: a commandment received directly from G-d. The biblical account of Abraham as the father of Judaism begins, appropriately, on the day that he was directed to embark on a journey that would culminate four-hundred years later at Sinai. Until that point, every one of Abraham's decisions had been influenced by his own convictions, understanding, and inclinations. This was the first time he followed a course of action out of *obedience* to a Higher Authority. This defined Abraham as a Jew, and this defines our Judaism as well.

Beyond philosophy and moral conviction, Judaism is about pure faith and simple obedience.[4]

Born with Abraham, molded at Sinai, our religion is enduring, with a unique obedience that is its central tenet.

---

[3] *Genesis* 12:1. See also *Genesis* 12:4. See Nachmanides on *Genesis* 12:2.

[4] This essay is based in part on Likutei Sichot, vol. XXV, p. 48.

"If we are meant to serve out of obedience rather than follow our understanding of things, why do we work so hard to understand the Torah?"

REACHING BEYOND

ASKING FOR HELP?

The Golden Menorah of the Tabernacle was built to a specific, but complex, design. G-d described the design to Moses, but Moses did not understand. G-d explained it again, and even drew a picture, but to no avail. Moses was still unable to understand. In the end, G-d instructed Moses to toss the gold into the fire and the Menorah would miraculously emerge.[1] Since G-d knew that He would eventually have to make it Himself, why did He enlist Moses' help, in the first place?

A simpler question is: What was so difficult about the design that G-d, the greatest Teacher of all time, could not make Moses, the greatest student of all time, comprehend?

The Mystics explain that Moses actually understood the design. What he failed to comprehend was why these separate components — seven branches and forty-nine adornments — had to be chiselled from a single slab of gold. Plurality (of the adornments) and singularity (of the gold slab) are opposites. That they should be wed defies human understanding.[2]

BEYOND HUMAN GRASP

To help us understand the relationship between the forty-nine adornments and the single slab of gold, we turn to another concept that is related to the number forty-nine: the counting of the Omer.

The seven branches and forty-nine adornments of the Menorah correspond to the seven weeks, forty-nine days, between Passover, when our ancestors

---

[1] Tanchuma *Shemini* 3 and *Bamidbar Rabbah* 15:4. See also Rashi and Ramban on *Exodus* 28:31 and on *Numbers* 8:4.

[2] Sefer Halikutim, Erech Menorah, p. 861. For a slightly different interpretation, see Likutei Sichot, Vol. I, p. 174.

left Egypt, and Shavuot, when they received the Torah at Sinai. The Torah instructs us to count the days of this seven-week period, which amounts to forty-nine days. Yet in a separate verse, the Torah instructs us to count fifty days. How can we count fifty days in a forty-nine-day period? The Jewish mystics tell us that the fiftieth day was counted by G-d when He gave us the Torah.[3]

Receiving the Torah requires forty-nine steps of preparation. Every word of the Torah is of such complex wisdom that it can be understood in forty-nine different ways. It requires tremendous diligence to comprehend and internalize such depth. Our scholarship of Torah must grow every day until we reach the highest wisdom accessible to the human mind. The forty-nine-day count thus represents our quest for Torah wisdom.

There is another element in Torah that is beyond our intellectual grasp, namely, G-d, its Author. The Torah's information can be grasped intellectually, but attaching ourselves to it its Author requires humility. The intellect cannot connect us to G-d, because G-d transcends the human mind. Only humility can bind us to G-d.

This bond is represented by the number fifty, the day that transcends the forty-nine steps of human comprehension. The fiftieth day is the day that only G-d can count, it represents the Divine nature of the Torah's Authorship, which transcends our grasp. We cannot reach it by ourselves. Yet, if we count for forty-nine days, if we apply ourselves to the forty-nine perspectives or facets of Torah that are accessible to the human mind, G-d bestows the fiftieth from Above.

The fiftieth perspective sheds a new light on the original forty-nine. For forty-nine days, we understood them as forty-nine unique approaches. On the fiftieth day, we realize that all forty-nine perspectives flow from a common foundation, namely the fiftieth that is bestowed from Above. This single kernel of Divine wisdom shines through a prism of forty-nine colors. In the

---

[3] Likutei Torah *Bamidbar* 10.

REACHING FOR G-D

beginning, we saw only forty-nine colors. On the fiftieth day, we discern their Single Source. We cannot arrive at this wisdom on our own; we receive it from G-d, Who bestows it from Above.

BECOMING A VESSEL

If the goal of Torah study is to connect to its Author and thus understand the fiftieth perspective, and if such connection can be bestowed only from Above, why do we need to study the Torah? Why does G-d not bestow understanding from Above? In other words, what do the forty-nine steps accomplish, if they fail to catapult us to the fiftieth?

They turn us into recipients. G-d does not want scholars; He wants students. He does not want accomplished teachers; He wants elevated souls. He doesn't want our profound comprehension; He wants our transformed characters. G-d's purpose is that we become vessels and conduits for His holiness. And to do that, we must apply ourselves. The toil, the yearning, the desperate, earnest desire for G-d turns an ego into a vessel. This is accomplished through the forty-nine-day effort.[4]

ELEGANCE OF SINGULARITY

We now return to the Menorah. Its forty-nine adornments were beautiful and meaningful. Their graceful forms, flowing symmetry, profound meaning and symbolism inspired Moses to great passion. Each was significant, each contributed, and each deserved its own place. "Why must they all be chiseled from a single slab of gold?!" his sensitive soul cried. "Why blemish their distinctive beauty by the stark uniformity of a single slab?"

---

[4] See Sefat Emet, 1871 and Maharal al Hatorah, *Exodus* 28:31. See also *Babylonian Talmud; Eiruvin* 13b that *Sumchus* proposed forty-eight arguments to declare something pure and forty-eight arguments to declare it impure. It can be argued that the first forty-eight perspectives of Torah are countered by parallel perspectives of impurity. The forty-ninth perspective, though it too is countered by an impure perspective, is able to transcend its opponent and render us vessels for Divinity.

The adornments were unique, and Moses grieved for the loss of a pluralism that he felt should have been celebrated. Pluralism and singularity are polar opposites; only G-d can wed them. Only G-d could demonstrate that the forty-nine separate adornments are, in fact, manifestations of a single kernel of Divine beauty. Moses understood the forty-nine adornments, but the one slab of gold was the secret of the fiftieth, a secret only G-d could understand.

No explanation could make Moses understand. Yet over and over again, G-d tried to explain it and Moses tried to grasp it. Why? Because only after Moses made the effort with such terrific diligence was he worthy of receiving the fiftieth perspective. Only after he tried to understand, but failed, did G-d make the Menorah Himself and share the secret of the fiftieth perspective.

Our approach to Torah reflects Moses' experience with the Menorah. We study it and toil mightily to understand. We achieve a small measure of success, each according to his abilities. But the degree of our understanding is not as important as the sincerity of our efforts. When we apply ourselves to the Torah, with sincere yearning for closeness to G-d, we become worthy recipients, even conduits, of the Divine, holy aura.[5]

In this way, the way of effort — and only in this way — do we transcend our comprehension of Torah and forge a connection with G-d.

---

[5] See *Shemot Rabbah* 36:2–3. See also *Bamidbar Rabbah* 15:4–5.

"But is G-d interested only in our serving and connecting with Him? Doesn't He care about us, and our interests?

LIBERTY AND MISERY
EDICTS AND REWARDS
Judaism is replete with Divine edicts and commandments, some of which we understand, many of which we don't, but all of which we are required to fulfill. These commandments cover nearly every facet of human life. From waking to sleeping, from the way we dress to the way we eat, everything is governed by religious law. Everything must be done in accordance with G-d's Will. But what of *our* will? Aren't we important too?

HEALTHY DISCIPLINE
Not all freedoms are beneficial to us. Being governed by a firm set of rules can actually be to our benefit. Children are a wonderful example.

Our children are ruled by a strict regimen. We give them curfew hours and nonnegotiable bedtimes; we require them to eat balanced, nutritious meals. Children often feel constricted by these rules. They are jealous of those whose parents allow them to come and go as they please, eat as they choose, and miss school whenever they feel like it. As adults, we know better. Caring parents enforce discipline, because it is better for their children. Parents who love their children and want them to develop properly offer a healthy mix of discipline and love.

In some ways, we are all children. Being governed by G-d's Law is to our cosmic benefit. That G-d constructed a system of law to guide us demonstrates His profound love for us. It demonstrates how much we mean to Him. It demonstrates that He cares.

EMPATHETIC CONCERN
The intricate attachments of marriage are often seen by singles as burdensome. In a marriage, husbands and wives call each other regularly just to check in. Many single men and women view this as a sacrifice of carefree liberty. Unmarried, they are free to go as they please, whereas in marriage

their spouses would want to know where they go, what they do, how they travel, and when they arrive. It could seem stifling.

But most married people say that they view this attachment as a gift. When spouses ask each other to call, they are really saying that they're worried and that they care. When we are single, no one bothers us about where we're going, because no one cares. Whether we have a wonderful day or a miserable day, there will be no one at home to share our frustrations and joys. We could get lost and no one would be the wiser. We could find our way home and no one would rejoice. No one would know because no one would care enough to find out. In marriage, we have a partner who cares for us. No matter where we are, our spouse will think of us and worry about our welfare. "Call me," she'll say. What she's really saying is, *"I love you."* "Call me," he'll say. What he's really saying is, *"You matter to me."*

AIMLESS WANDERER

I remember reading a story about someone who faked his own death and moved to a distant country, under an assumed name. At first, his newfound anonymity seemed liberating and his freedom exhilarating. But after several days, he understood the bitter price he had paid. He could go where he pleased, because no one cared. He could live or he could die — no one would care. No one knew who he was. He mattered to absolutely no one.

DIVINE EDICTS

We now return to our initial question: Are our desires important to G-d? Are *we* important to G-d?

If we were in fact meaningless to G-d, if He didn't care about our spiritual and cosmic welfare, He would have left us to our own devices. He would have allowed us to roam through life at our leisure. It wouldn't have mattered if we were moral, faithful, or observant. "Do what you want," He would say. "You're meaningless to Me."

But actually, He loves us and cares for us. He worries for us and is concerned with our behavior. Our successes elate Him and our failures distress Him. We matter to Him. We are His children, and like a loving parent, He says, "I can't just forget about you and let you do as you wish — I love you." Like a concerned spouse, He says, "I care about you. Call Me when you cross the street, and call Me when you arrive. I want to hear from you every day. In fact, at least three times a day."

If He left us alone and did not care, we would not be free. A lonely existence is a crushing burden. It constrains us and robs us of freedom. True freedom, the kind of freedom that allows our souls to soar, comes from knowing that we matter enough to make a difference. That we are important enough to make a difference.

IN CONCLUSION

G-d's commandments do not rob us of our essential significance. On the contrary, they endow us with our essential significance. What could feel better than to know that I — little insignificant me — am important to an infinite and eternal G-d?

Would we feel freer if we were permitted to go where we pleased and do what we pleased? Perhaps, in the short term. But after a while, we would feel constrained. Entrapped by our own insignificance, we would pine for the freedom that comes with validation. [1]

What better way to free our personality from the crushing weight of meaningless isolation than to be told that we matter on a cosmic scale?

---

[1] This essay is based on a lecture by Rabbi Y. Y. Jacobson. To view the lecture, visit *www.tiferes.org/4archives.htm.*

"All right, so G-d cares about me. But can't I, and my actions and life, be meaningful to G-d without committing to living according to Torah?"

INFINITESIMAL SPECK

GREATER THAN LIFE

Do you ever get the feeling that you are but an infinitesimal speck, swallowed by the vastness of the universe and beyond, that cosmic forces arrayed along your path lead you to a destiny greater than your imagination, that life as you know it barely scratches the surface?

MOSES AND WATER

The name "Moses" means "drawn forth," in Hebrew. Moses was thus called because, as an infant, he was drawn forth from the waters of the Nile.[1] The Jewish mystics saw water as a symbol of Divinity. That Moses was drawn from water indicates that his soul was from a transcendental, spiritual realm, far beyond our scope of comprehension.[2]

Many key periods of Moses' life were associated with water. He met his wife at a well, and drew water for her. G-d identified him as the shepherd of Israel, when he stood by a brook till his sheep drank their fill. He led his people during the Splitting of the Reed Sea. He was forbidden to enter into the Land of Israel because of an incident related to water.[3] These episodes are described in the Torah in great detail.

The Torah doesn't relate historical incidents for the sake of keeping a historical record, but rather, always to teach us something. The Jewish mystics

---

[1] *Exodus* 2:10. Fearing infanticide, his mother, *Yocheved*, hid him from the Egyptian authorities. She placed him in a basket and set the basket upon the Nile. An Egyptian princess found him and rescued him. She called him Moses, because she drew him forth from the waters of the Nile.

[2] Torah Ohr, *Shemot* 51b. See also *U'sh'avtem Mayim Besasson* 5621. Note also that the prophet Isaiah spoke of a day when the world will fill with knowledge of G-d as waters cover the seabed.

[3] *Exodus* 2:15–21. *Shemot Rabbah* 2:2. *Exodus* 14:15. *Number* 19:4–14.

explained that in drawing water for his future wife, and by association, for us, Moses, man of G-d, manifested an awareness of G-d, otherwise prevalent only in the higher realms. He taught us that life without G-d is as insignificant as one droplet of water in a vast ocean filled with water.[4]

BUSY DROPLETS

Our entire universe, our activities, concerns, indeed our very selves, are but a drop in G-d's great ocean. There are billions of aqua bits in the ocean, one droplet is insignificant. Yet, each droplet is a universe unto itself. Each contain molecules, atoms, oxygen, hydrogen, protons, neutrons, electrons, and quarks.

It is only a droplet, but it is a "beehive" of molecular activity. Each droplet contains millions of molecules. To the molecules, the droplet seems as vast as the universe itself. Each molecule forms electrostatic associations with other molecules. Negative hydrogen protons in one molecule bond with positive oxygen protons in other molecules. The bonding process is constant, as protons form and dissolve their associations. Should these associations cease for even one moment, the entire droplet would disintegrate.

Not only is there intense activity between molecules, each molecule is itself filled with activity. Electrons orbit in dizzying, but indeterminate, patterns. Hydrogen protons share their electrons with oxygen protons. Should a proton have one too many, or one too few, electrons, the entire molecule would destabilize. From time to time, a hydrogen proton in one molecule jumps over into another molecule. This too destabilizes the molecule and sends it into a frenzied search for a replacement.

---

[4] Likutei Torah, *Bamidbar* 88b. The *Zohar* describes Moses as a faithful shepherd (*Zohar* III 225b). The Chassidic masters went one step further and described him as a shepherd of faith. He formulated and fortified Israel's faith in G-d. See Sefer Hamaamarim 5687, p. 113.

Unimportant Molecules

If molecules could talk they would speak of their hectic days and of their frantic efforts to balance their countless needs. To hear them tell it, their contribution is critical and indispensable. Unfortunately for them, water drop-droplets really don't matter. At the end of the day, they're just a bunch of molecules. If they have the temerity to appear on our kitchen counter or mahogany table, we simply wipe them dry. Millions of molecules wiped away, with a casual swipe of the hand.

But don't tell that to the molecule! Its atoms would be incensed! They devote their entire existence to stabilizing the droplet's chemical balance, and we suggest that they're meaningless? Yet when the molecular system of one droplet fails to right itself, the oceans don't dry out and our water supply is not endangered. In the greater scheme of things, these molecules are unimportant.

Our Own Little Droplets

Are we any different? We scurry about all day, solving problems and putting out fires, working to balance our many needs. We provide for our family, raise our children, and rise to social prominence. We consider ourselves important, in fact, nearly indispensable. Yet the truth is that we are, from G-d's perspective, a mere droplet in the ocean. Our material failures and successes do not have any impact on G-d's cosmic and true Existence. Material success, military victories, diplomatic triumphs, and academic excellence are, within the bubble of our little droplet, legitimate aspirations. But on G-d's plane they are trivial. G-d is as removed from such aspirations as we are from water molecules. No matter how high we rise in commercial, diplomatic, or academic stratospheres, our success is insignificant in the eyes of the Divine.

By drawing water, Moses demonstrated that we are but a molecule in G-d's eyes. He engendered within us a yearning for G-d — a yearning to harness our material gains in the service of G-d and thus give cosmic meaning to our otherwise temporal existence, a yearning to serve a purpose greater than ourselves, a yearning for a truly meaningful life.

Without G-d, of what significance is our existence? We are but a drop-let. But when it is connected to G-d, by adherence to His word, even a mere droplet like us is filled with meaning.

"So living for a Divine purpose grants us significance and validation. Sure, I want those things. But what about … happiness?"

Freedom to Eat
The Buffet Dilemma

You are standing in front of a heaping buffet that is laden with mouthwatering delicacies. Your appetite is stimulated. The host grants you carte blanche, freedom to indulge. Stop for a moment. Are you really free? With your plate piled high and your appetite running into overdrive, you take your first bite. Delicious! There's nothing like it. But the second bite isn't quite so pleasurable. The third bite is even less of a thrill, and it's all downhill from there.

Standing there in front of the buffet, imagine the next morning. You can't fit into your clothing. You feel swollen and cramped, and you berate yourself for having eaten too much. So let us repeat the question: Are you really free? Have you no one to answer to? You *do* have a master and that master is *yourself*.

Dieting

When I was on a diet, I trained myself to eschew the crass temptations of bagels and lox. On Sunday morning, the entire congregation would tear into their breakfast with relish. I would sip my water and pick at my apple. They all regarded me with pity. Only I knew better. It was I who pitied them. When they looked at their plate they saw a culinary delight. When I looked at the bagels, I saw a gluttonous nightmare that, if I ate, I would pay for in spades. They walked away with a satisfied smile; I walked away with a sense of achievement. I had made a lasting contribution to my health and to my waistline. Three hours later, I was out jogging and they were nursing stomach cramps.

In retrospect, who was really free that morning? I find it amusing that, when tempted by a second helping, we often allow ourselves the *freedom* of indulgence. Are we offering ourselves freedom or bondage? Are we free to indulge or free of indulgence? Which is more rewarding? Who is more free?

THE PARADOX

It is human nature, evidenced in all areas of life: A corporate executive is a slave to his desk, telephone, BlackBerry, and, of course, customers. Every day is a pressure cooker; he craves a vacation. He finally breaks with routine and flies out to a remote island to relax. He lies on the beach and wiggles his toes for a couple of days — and suddenly, he can't stand the boredom. He wants his office back.

The phenomenon is even more complex. The high-powered corporate executive is jealous of the simple island dweller who lives in quiet serenity. Yet the island dweller would like nothing better than to abandon his island and move to the city, where he might become an important corporate executive! The executive can't wait to get out onto the island to taste the life of freedom. The island dweller feels chained to the island and pines for the freedom of the city. Who is right? Where does true freedom lie?

PURPOSE

Former American President Richard Nixon once observed that many people yearn for the luxuries that are readily available to the wealthy. They want the freedom to golf, patronize expensive restaurants, attend the theater, and travel the world. This dream is meaningful to almost everyone, with the exception of those who have already attained it. To them it is meaningless.

They have discovered that meaning cannot be found in comfort or luxury. Meaning can be found only in purpose. To live a purposeful life and to make a difference is meaningful. Yet when the wealthy grow poor and are forced to give up the luxuries to which they have grown accustomed, they pine for their former luxuries. They who have discovered true meaning pine for creature comforts. Why?

Those granted luxury, pine for purpose. Those blessed with purpose, pine for luxury. Which is correct?

DUALITY OF LIFE

Life is a duel between our surface and inner dimensions. On the surface, we seek instant gratification, be it by means of food, luxury, or freedom; we are dissatisfied unless we achieve our material and immediate goals. But once we achieve them, a deeper dissatisfaction sets in. It is the dissatisfaction of the soul. The soul is not appeased by transient gratification; the soul seeks meaning. The lifelong quest for meaning leads us to demand much from ourselves, for true meaning cannot be achieved without sacrifice. Yet, in sacrifice, we lose something of our surface gratification, which leads to dissatisfaction all over again. So the cycle continues. We cannot invest in one end without divesting from the other.

Balance cannot be found in shifting loyalties that drive us unmercifully to and fro. Are we meant to hover between the two extremes, tempted to land in either, but forever trapped in the futile center?

KOSHER

Rather than viewing the inner and surface dimensions as polar extremes, Judaism views them as alternate sides of the same spectrum. A life of purpose might be lived selfishly and a life of indulgence might be lived purposefully. The key is not to look at what we do, as much as at why we do it.

Our quest for meaning leads in many directions. It is often translated as making a contribution. It is also translated as being needed by someone. Sometimes it is said that purpose in life is achieved through leaving our mark on the world after we have departed from it.

From a religious standpoint, the highest calling of purpose is to leave the Creator's imprint on His creation. In this way we leave not only our own mark, but that of G-d. G-d's mark is imprinted when we interact with the world around us and engage in it on His terms, in accordance with His wishes.

The kosher dietary laws distinguish the foods we are permitted to eat from the foods we are not permitted to eat. This diet enables us to serve G-d and endow our lives with meaning even as we enjoy its delicacies. We are not forced to choose between purpose and satisfaction; we incorporate both at once. We choose the dishes that we like to eat, but ascertain that they are kosher, because G-d has commanded it that way. We go on vacation to serve ourselves, but choose our location in accordance with how and where G-d's wishes are best served. We thus endow our surface dimension with inner meaning.

We could choose to serve only ourselves and eat to our heart's content, but life would lose all meaning. We could choose to forgo all foods and serve only G-d, but that wouldn't be satisfying. The key is to remember that we can serve G-d through eating just as much as we can serve Him through abstaining. At work and on vacation, the corporate executive and the island dweller, both find purpose and satisfaction.

Living for a meaningful purpose bestows happiness too.

"Are we really one large family? Because it seems to me that some Jews think they are more important than others?"

EVERY JEW IS CRUCIAL
WHY?

"Why am I seen, in certain Jewish circles, as a lesser Jew — as somehow inferior? After all, I was born to a Jewish mother, though I don't practice Judaism on a very high level. Am I any less Jewish?"

I could see the pain in his eyes as he repeated the hurtful words, and I too felt a twinge of sadness. Trying to comfort him, I said, "Try to forget what they said. You don't live in their neighborhood, and you don't attend those synagogues. Luckily, you live in a more understanding community."

"But," he rightly protested, "the Jewish People are a single entity. If some Jews are disconnected from others, I can't relax simply because I'm not immediately affected."

His words cut to the heart of the matter. I acknowledged that he was correct. We are one People, one body, and if one piece is missing, the entire bloc is affected. It is true that all Jews are equally obligated to observe the Torah. But it is also true that those who don't observe are full and equal members of the Jewish community. After all, every Jew is G-d's cherished child. Every Jew is integral to the Chosen Nation.

DIAMONDS

Rabbi Menachem M. Schneersohn, the Lubavitcher Rebbe, would stand for hours to greet Jews from all walks of life who came to see him. He was elderly, no longer endowed with the energy of youth. Someone once asked him, "Don't you ever tire?"

"Every Jew is a diamond," the Rebbe replied. "One never tires of counting diamonds."

The Rebbe's response seemed more poetic than practical. Is every Jew truly a diamond? What of the criminals? What of the insensitive, arrogant, and conceited Jews? What of the Jews who are completely oblivious to Torah?

The prophet Isaiah wrote of the Jewish People: "This is the nation I have formed for [the service of] Myself. My praises they shall tell."[1] What an interesting statement. G-d formed the Jewish People for Himself, for His purposes. How do we serve G-d's purpose? One would assume that we serve G-d through prayer, Torah study, and observance of the *mitzvot*.

But that's not what the prophet says! This nation serves Me even before they sing My praises. The prophet doesn't say that G-d formed the nation so that they could sing His praises. He said that the Jew was formed for G-d. Period. That the Jew sings G-d's praises is added later, almost as an afterthought.

SUBJECTS TO THE KING
The very existence of a Jew — even one who does not pray, study, or observe the commandments — is a testament to G-d's greatness. G-d is our King, and we are first and foremost His subjects.

A king cannot reign unless there is a nation over whom to reign. The very existence of subjects makes him a sovereign. Even a subject who does not obey the king's law makes a contribution as a member of the nation. Though every nation has its nobility and its commoners, the monarchy is not truly a monarchy if it is accepted only by the nobility. Acceptance by the entire nation, the ministers, nobility, and the commoners, is what makes it a monarchy. Every common subject, even the criminal, contributes to help make it a kingdom.[2]

---

[1] *Isaiah* 43:21.

[2] Though we chant every morning (in Adon Olam) that G-d was King before all creatures were created, we mean that he was King in His Essence, since Kingship is one of His Divine attributes. His actual reign over mankind began when He created Adam and Eve. See Sefer Mamarim 5703, p. 10

The Jewish People also have nobility and commoners. The righteous and pious, our scholars and sages, are our nobility. But the pious cannot alone
comprise a kingdom. For G-d to be king over a nation, the common Jew as
much as the pious Jew is required, the nonobservant as much as the observant. One Jew is not intrinsically greater than another. From this point of
view, we are all equal.

"This is the nation that I have formed for [the service of] Myself." Even before we sing His praises, our very existence constitutes His kingdom. We
each serve equally in this great purpose.

We Can ... and Must

This fact does not exempt us from Torah and *mitzvot*. It doesn't justify lack of
observance on the part of any Jew. It simply means that no Jew can discount
another, regardless of background, observance, or affiliation, for we each
play a significant role.[3]

---

[3] In addition to making up G-d's kingdom, every Jew is also a living testament to
G-d's love for the Jewish People, and to His power to dictate the course of history. The continued existence of our People is one of the greatest miracles of all
time. This is especially true of our generation, the sons and daughters of Holo-
caust survivors. Every Jew today is a walking testament to G-d's greatness and
love — testifying to this effect by his very existence, regardless of his level of Torah observance. No Jew has the right to dismiss another, because when we
dismiss another Jew, we dismiss a testament to G-d.

It's true that Torah law mandates the public shaming of sinners, in order to dis-
courage people from sin. When a person knows that his sins will be publicly
disclosed, he will be deterred from sinning. However, very strict criteria greatly
limit the application of this law. The details are too numerous to discuss here, but
these criteria include an obligation to first approach the sinner with love and
concern, to warn him and to try many times to dissuade him from sin, not aban-
doning hope after one or two attempts. One is also required to recruit to this
cause those who might influence the sinner for the better. Most importantly, it
includes an obligation to carefully consider all consequences before revealing a

Some Jews weren't raised with Torah. Others were raised with Torah, but were, unfortunately, exposed to negative experiences that turned them away from Torah. Such Jews might think that they are either exempt from, or incapable of, returning to the path of Torah, to the path of singing G-d's praises. Then we read that the prophet says, "My praises they shall sing." Every Jew is important; every Jew is crucial; and every Jew could, should, and will sing G-d's praises. We are fortunate to have been granted special status. We are fortunate to have been granted a Jewish soul. The prophets tell us that we have the potential and the obligation to nurture our soul and to bring it back to full expression.

We could bring out the best in ourselves. Furthermore, we could help to bring out the best in others. We could bring out the best in observant Jews by teaching them how to enhance their love and respect for all Jews. We could bring out the best in Jews who are not yet observant by demonstrating the beauty and warmth of authentic Torah Judaism.

FAMILY COHESIVENESS

This cannot be accomplished in an atmosphere of divisiveness and mistrust. We must approach every Jew with love and acceptance. We must treat every Jew with the respect that a G-dly prince or princess deserves. We must cher-

---

private fact to the public. Will such a revelation inspire the sinner to repent and change his ways? Or will it cause him to resent Torah and its ways?

In olden days, when the Jewish community was the only social outlet for a Jew, public shaming would often compel him to repent. Today, Jews who are publicly shamed are usually driven further away from Judaism. Those whose motives are not kosher, who are not motivated by pure love and a sincere desire to help the sinner repent, must refrain from such undertakings. Rather than chastising others, such Jews should work to increase their love for all Jews. See Tanya, ch. 32. Also, "Peace is the greatest vessel for blessing" (*Mishnah, Uktzin* 3:12). When we achieve unity and peace, we merit an additional measure of G-d's blessing.

ish every Jew, for all are G-d's children. We must love every Jew, for we are all one family.[4]

When contemplating the misbehavior of other Jews, our struggles to overcome our own weaknesses lend perspective. Though it's our nature to be quick to judge, we know from our own experience that no Jew should be judged by his outer actions. Above all, we must remember that every Jew plays a crucial role in the Divine master plan.[5]

---

[4] The only kind of Jew we must hate with a passion is the heretic. However only one who has studied the entire Torah and rejected it is a heretic. Those who are ignorant of Torah are not heretical; they must be nurtured and taught, not hated. Furthermore, heretics must also be loved. We must hate them with one side of our heart and love them with the other. See Tanya, chapter 32.

[5] This essay is based on a talk given by Rabbi Menachem M. Schneerson, the Lubavitcher Rebbe, on Nissan 3, 5751.

"I hear what you're saying about my inherent value, and the inherent value of each individual Jew. Is there collective value in a unified Jewish nation?"

DYING FOR LIFE

A HORRIBLE DILEMMA

A mother and son in a concentration camp. The boy is directed to the gas chamber; the mother is sentenced to life. She watches her child, forlorn and alone, as he walks to his death. Should she reject life to embrace her child or abandon her child to embrace life?

The mother who embraces life validates her child's heroism by contributing to life. Had the child's death triggered his mother's death it would have been a double tragedy.

Parents forced to make such agonizing decisions are liable to feel guilty for having abandoned their child. Yet the surviving parent must remember that his or her survival is precisely what the deceased child would have wanted. One's survival validates the other's sacrifice. If both had died it would have constituted an abandonment of the cause for which they died.

THREE ANNOUNCEMENTS

Before our ancestors would mobilize for war, they were addressed by a priest. The priest would offer words of encouragement and confident assurances of victory: "Let your heart not be faint; do not fear the enemy nor enter into panic. And do not be terrified, for G-d will vanquish your enemy for you."

They were then addressed by military officers, who would announce: "Any man who has built a home but has yet to live in it, planted a vineyard but has yet to render it fit for use, betrothed a woman but has yet to marry her, should return home, lest he die in war."[1]

---

[1] *Deuteronomy* 1:9.

This is an astounding time for such an announcement. The priest had just bolstered the morale of the troops, and the officers now set out to demoralize them by thinning their ranks and warning them of death! But, on reflection, a deeper meaning emerges that justifies the timing and tenor of these announcements.[2]

PROTECTING A WAY OF LIFE

The Talmud remarks that the order of these announcements reflects the order of life. First we build a home, then plant a vineyard or establish alternative sources of income, and only then should we marry.[3] This Talmud-

---

[2] There are many explanations offered by the commentaries. Two compelling arguments are presented here: Ibn Ezra argued that this was strategically wise. A man with such concerns on his mind will worry about his affairs at home and will be unable to keep his mind on the battle. Filling their ranks with such unmotivated troops would weaken the military and undermine their prospects for victory. Abarbanel argued that since these men had not yet had the opportunity to fulfill the respective *mitzvot* associated with their endeavor (the house builder has yet to build his parapet, the vineyard planter has yet to offer the priestly gifts, and the betrothed has yet to father children) they would not merit the miracles required for victory.

[3] *Babylonian Talmud, Sotah* 44a. See Maharsha, ibid., that this standard applied only to a person of means. One who cannot afford to build his own house and business may marry on the basis that the community will support him till he finds an independent source of income. *Yad Hachazakah, Hilchot Deiot* 5:1 puts house building ahead of vineyard planting. Many commentators have attempted to explain the seeming contradiction with the Talmudic statement. Torat Moshe on *Deuteronomy* 20:9 posits that since the Torah was actually referring to a vineyard that was already three years old (since the planter could not partake of his grapes till after the three years; see *Leviticus* 19:23–25), the house must have been built three years after the vineyard was planted. See also the verse quoted in the following footnote, where the order of house building and vineyard planting are reversed.

ic statement indicates that our Sages viewed these three announcements as a reflection on the ordinary routine of life.[4]

Why does an army go to war? To protect its national interest. What is a nation's primary interest? Its citizens' unhindered pursuit of life's ordinary routine. When an enemy threatens the ordinary pursuit of day-to-day life, the nation's very fabric is undermined. This was the very point that the officers communicated through their announcements.

The officers were not attempting to thin the army's ranks; on the contrary, they rallied the troops by restating their exalted purpose. Why are we going to war? To enable our nation to pursue life and its normal routines. To ensure their freedom to build homes, plant vineyards, and establish families. The troops were further reminded that these core values were not theoretical, but real. They were not only going to protect the freedom of nameless and faceless members of their nation; they were going to protect the freedom of their own comrades. If any of their comrades needed to complete his home, vineyard, or first year of marriage, these troops would fight to enable this.

But the comrades who were sent home to build their houses, vineyards, and families had not needed to respond to the draft in the first place; they were entitled to stay at home and claim a valid deferment. They came anyway. Why? Because how could they not come? How could they sit at home while their brothers risked life and limb for their country.

Yet, once they got there, they were told to go home. Like the mother who embraced life while her son walked off to the gas chambers, these soldiers, with their departure, validated their comrades' efforts on the battlefields. If they went to war, if they abandoned their routine, the enemy would have

---

[4] It is interesting to note that when G-d reprimands the Jews and warns of impending punishment if they abandon the Torah, the loss of these three freedoms are specified: "You will betroth a woman, but another man will lie with her; you will build a house, but another man will live in it; you will plant a vineyard, but will not render it fit for use (Deuteronomy 28:30).

won and their comrades would die in vain. It was not easy for them to abandon their brothers and go home. But sometimes abandonment is the highest form of embrace. This was one such case.

MODERN APPLICATION

When the enemies of Israel threaten our cities and population centers, when they send our citizens to bomb shelters and destroy our way of life, our nation is justified in going to war. Such war must be pursued until its goals are achieved. The war must continue until the routine of life is once again established, without fear of reprisal. If our soldiers are not safe, if our borders are being violated, and if our cities are under attack, our war is not over.

We mourn the loss of innocent lives on all sides. Our Torah ethic demands that. Yet we must pursue the war with persistence till peace is restored. Our Torah ethic demands that, too. We must not seek a peace that will lead to another war. We must seek a war that will lead to a lasting peace. This is the unfortunate reality foisted on us by our enemy.

FEAR NOTHING BUT SIN

Just before the army embarked on war, one last announcement was made: "He who is fearful and fainthearted should return home, lest he melt his brothers' heart as he melted his own."[5] There are those who fear war, but such fear cannot be tolerated during a war. The Torah instructs us to keep such fears silent, lest they melt the hearts of the brave.

According to one of our Sages, this announcement was directed to sinners. He who is fearful on account of his sins should return home, lest he jeopardize the entire army.[6] The lesson to our era is clear. Israel's destiny is in G-d's hands and our enemies need be feared only if our sins render us unworthy of Divine protection. We must arm our troops with proper weaponry and adequate training, but in the end, our fate lies with G-d. So long as we place our

---

[5] *Deuteronomy* 1:9.

[6] *Babylonian Talmud, Sotah* 44a. See also Rashi and Nachmanides on *Deuteronomy* 20:9.

REACHING FOR G-D

trust in G-d, we have no reason to fear our enemy. The only thing we have to fear is sin.

Life is a worthy cause, worthy enough to die for. But we succeed only because our brother's life is as important to us as our own. This is the inherent unity of the Jewish nation. One Jew dies so that another will live; and when the latter lives, s/he lives for both.

"You say there is 'inherent unity in the Jewish nation'? If we're so unified, why are we always fighting each other?"

Unity – in Good Times and Bad
Danger Brings Us Together

Disaster is the parent of opportunity. When the normal routine is shaken, when calm and confidence are shattered, the patterns of life are altered and new opportunities are born. It remains to us to convert these opportunities into reality. It remains to us to grasp that if we do our part, even dark clouds can have a silver lining.

In May of 1967, the worldwide Jewish community joined, in a unity unprecedented in modern times, to face the grave danger that threatened Israel. Personal animosities and parochial differences were set aside. Longstanding fissures were instantly resolved, longstanding grudges were, at least for the moment, summarily dismissed. Because we realized that the enemy did not discriminate; he threatened the entire community. And this realization brought us together.

Jews who had never thought about visiting Israel before traveled en masse to volunteer their help. Jews secure in distant countries contributed their life savings in defense of the Land. The impending crisis brought to the fore a devotion we never knew we possessed. An otherwise fragmented people was forced by a common enemy to find common ground. The threat of incredible disaster gave rise to an incredible opportunity for unity and love. At that moment, our unity was total.

Fertile, But Foreign, Lands

As our ancestors approached the Promised Land, two tribes sought permission to settle in the fertile, but foreign, lands outside of the Land of Israel. Moses acquiesced, with one stipulation. He asked that they join the Jewish army in times of war.[1]

---

[1] *Numbers* 22.

I would like to offer a different perspective. Moses sought to determine the mindset of these two tribes, who were prepared, in pursuit of material gain, to break with their brethren. Did they still see themselves as members of the Jewish nation? Or was the promise of bounty on the Jordan's East Bank causing them to sever their ties with the Jewish nation?

The only litmus test that could prove their loyalty was their behavior during times of war. With their families safely ensconced in another land, would they identify with their brethren in time of war? Would they risk life and limb to come to their brethren's aid? If they would draft an army and fight alongside their brethren, they would pass the litmus test and demonstrate true Jewish identity.

WHY DO WE WAIT?

In times of peace, they were content to pursue their selfish dreams, far from the rest of their brethren. The fact that Jewish unity would suffer did not concern them as much as their own well-being did.[2] Though they viewed themselves as a common people, their commonality did not emerge — until it was threatened by war.

It is true that disasters parent opportunities for unity and hope. But it is frustrating that, unfortunately, the other side of the coin is: it takes a disaster to bring us together. Why can't we stand together at all times? Why must we wait for a crisis to show our unity and common identity? Why can't we appreciate each other in peace as we do in war? Today, this goal, noble as it is, seems almost unreachable. But there will come a time when the astounding unity currently reserved for times of danger will become the norm.

NOAH AND THE MESSIANIC AGE

The prophet Isaiah promised that, in the Messianic age, animals of prey will abandon their ferocious natures. "The wolf shall lie down with the lamb, and the leopard with the goat; the calf, the cub, and the ox will sit together, and a

---

[2] This is why these tribes were the first Jews to be exiled from their Land. *Bamidbar Rabbah* 22. For a deeper perspective, see *Likutei Sichot* XIII, p. 189–191.

child will lead them. The cow and the bear will graze together; the lion and the cattle will both eat hay."[3]

This particular miracle has already occurred once before in history. In Noah's Ark, during the Flood, the wild animals curbed their aggression and got along. The lion did not prey on the sheep and the tiger did not stalk the lamb. Rabbi Yisrael Meir Lau, former chief rabbi of Israel, posed the following question: If, when it occurred in the Ark, this miracle did not herald the Messianic age, why was Isaiah convinced that the next time it occurred it would herald the Messianic age?[4]

In response, Rabbi Lau suggested, that a distinction can be drawn between Noah's Ark and the Messianic age.

The animals were gathered in Noah's Ark in order to survive the Flood; they needed to get along with each other in order to survive. If they would have turned on each other, they would have destroyed the Ark that offered them safe haven. They had to survive together or not at all. The lion's goodwill was thus intended to save himself; it was not for the sake of those around him. In the Messianic age there will not be a threat that will have to be survived. There will be no compelling reason for the docile nature of previously ferocious animals. Peace and security will arise not of necessity, but out of desire. Not out of tragedy, but out of goodwill. The animals will *choose* to become peaceful.

This is a phenomenon not extant today. But Isaiah prophesied that when we witness this astounding miracle, we will know with certainty that the Messianic age has arrived.[5]

In times of danger, the Jewish People unite like the family we truly are. In times of peace, this unity seems to slip away. When we learn to

---

[3] *Isaiah* 11:6–7.

[4] The chief rabbi's comments were delivered in Toronto on Monday, June 5, 2006.

[5] If we emulate that way of life today, we will hasten the arrival of the Messianic age.

REACHING FOR G-D

demonstrate the same unity in times of peace as we do in times of danger, we will know that the Moshiach has arrived. This will be a silver lining without the cloud. A time of true and total peace.

"I see what you mean by the inherent value of every Jew, and the need to defend all Jews and to reach out to them in love. But what happens when the Jew in question doesn't respond with love? How do I control my own emotions, when confronted with the hatred of those who try to harm me?"

THOSE WHO WOULD HARM US

TAKING OFFENSE

It takes years to gain maturity, but it seems to take only moments to discard it. We have all witnessed grown adults regressing into childish behavior when thrust into an argument. Insults are exchanged, tempers rise, and before anyone knows what's happened, otherwise mature adults are behaving like children.

Such behavior is easy to criticize when witnessed from the outside. But deep down, we know that we too are susceptible. We each have vulnerabilities that we don't want exposed. When these sensitivities are probed, we respond with passion and even immaturity. Emotional reactions are easily triggered, but very difficult to control. Yet the Torah expects us to do precisely that.

MOSES

Moses was an exemplary model of such inner discipline. Leaders are rarely without detractors, and in that regard, Moses was no different. Of his many detractors, *Datan* and *Abiram* stood out as intractable enemies. From the very beginning, these two men were the bane of Moses' existence. When he was a young prince, growing up in Pharaoh's palace, they betrayed his confidence and forced him to flee the country.[1] When Moses introduced the Heavenly manna to the Israelites, in the desert, these two men stirred up trouble by

---

[1] In the process of defending a Jew from Egyptian aggression, Moses killed an Egyptian slave driver. *Datan* and *Abiram* reported Moses to the authorities, and he was sentenced to death. See *Exodus* 2:11–16 and *Devarim Rabbah* 2:27 for details on Moses' miraculous escape.

challenging the rules under which the manna was offered.[2] *Datan* and *Abiram* used every opportunity to challenge Moses' authority. So when they joined *Korach's* rebellion against Moses it was hardly a surprise. Moses, in an incredible display of humility and self discipline, invited *Datan* and *Abiram* to dialogue with him. They mocked his invitation, but Moses didn't take offense. He saw that they wouldn't come to him so he patiently went to them.[3]

Moses, the leader of Israel, challenged repeatedly, had every right to cast them out and punish them. But he wouldn't hear of it. How did he achieve such self-discipline? What is the magic potion that counters the rise of the ego and enables such incredible self-effacement?

ANGER AND FAITH

There is, of course, no magic potion. It was no pill that Moses took, but the perspective he brought to his interaction with others. Our Sages equated anger with the cardinal sin of idolatry. Moses might have reasoned that since the sin of anger is so grievous as to be compared to idolatry and since we are required to sacrifice our lives to avoid idolatry, surely we are required to sacrifice our ego and rein in our tempers to avoid anger.[4]

But what is the connection between anger and idolatry? We must be prepared to die rather than abandon our faith. But to compare a rising temper with idolatrous worship, and to ask us to make a herculean effort to avoid anger as we would to avoid idolatry, requires an explanation.

THE MASTER PLAN

Divine Providence is a central tenet of our faith. We believe in a personal G-d, Who guides the universe and Who is intimately engaged in every facet of

---

[2] Moses relayed G-d's instructions that the manna must be consumed on the day it was collected. *Datan* and *Abiram* refused to accept this and challenged Moses. They deliberately left over manna for the next day, which putrified. See *Exodus* 16:20. *Shemot Rabbah* 25:10.

[3] Exodus 24:12–15; Exodus 24:25; *Midrash* Tanchuma; Parshat *Korach* 3.

[4] Babylonian Talmud, *Shabbat* 105b. Zohar, Genesis 27b.

our lives. We believe that if we are happy or sad, healthy or ill, wealthy or poor, He not only knows it, but actually orchestrates it.

We would not be poor if G-d did not will it, nor would we be wealthy if G-d did not will it. The doctrine of Divine Providence states that G-d is the Root Cause of everything, even the most seemingly insignificant details of our lives. Everything works in accordance with His grand design; nothing is co-incidental. G-d determines whether we catch the green light on our way home from work or get stuck at the red light. G-d determines whether we trip and stub our toe or make it home safely. The Divine master plan is all-encompassing, everything affects the overall scheme of history and creation. If we can't find our blue suit before an important meeting, there is a reason; so it was decreed at the moment of Creation. It may seem absurd to us that something so seemingly trivial could be part of a master plan, but that's only because we're not privy to Divine thought. If we could understand G-d's thoughts, we would understand why every detail matters.

A DIVINE AFFAIR

Since every occurrence has been deliberately planned and executed by G-d, there's no difference, in this regard, between foolishly stepping on our own toe or being insulted by someone else. Neither could have happened if G-d had not willed it. And since He did will it, who are we to object or take offense?[5]

The person who hurt me has free will; he may have used it to choose to hurt me (unless this was unintentional). G-d did not force him to slight me or strike me. But he couldn't have succeeded unless G-d had first decreed that (for some reason, related both to me and to my role in the Divine master plan) I was meant to be hurt today. This particular person didn't have to

---

[5] We surely have no cause to grow angry with G-d. G-d's Will is both the best possible thing that could transpire for our own personal growth, and at the same time, precisely what is needed for His master plan of Creation. Aiding the master plan of Creation is beneficial not only to all of creation, but also to us. In a roundabout way, our own pain comes back to benefit us personally.

choose to be the one to become the executor of G-d's plan, but why he made such a choice is between him and G-d. He will have to account for his choice before G-d, but that is neither my affair nor my concern. I have no cause to be upset with him over that. I cannot blame him because I was hurt today. He could not have accomplished that if G-d had not willed it. I can "blame" Only G-d.

Blaming the instrument of my pain and growing angry with him, is tantamount to denying the Divine origin of this event. It is like banishing G-d from this occurrence, and declaring that He had no hand in it. But G-d is omnipresent, and cannot be banished from any time or space. Denying this is, in a word, heresy. It is tantamount to idolatry, which is why our Sages compared the two.[6]

We now see why Moses never grew angry over *Datan* and *Abiram's* audacity. He was dismayed by their taunts, but he knew that his distress served a Heavenly cause. Moses never took *Datan* and *Abiram's* insolence personally. That was between them and G-d. Rather than anger toward them, Moses felt compassion.

Our every footstep reflects the Divine master plan. Do we have time for petty anger and revenge?

---

[6] For further elucidation, see Iggeret Hakodesh 25.

"You speak of Jewish unity, but first we must identify as Jews. How does one do that in the Diaspora?"

WHERE AM I?

THE LOST CHILD

When I was younger, my father often told me about the little boy who never got to school on time. There was always something missing, and the boy was constantly scurrying about to find it. If it wasn't his pants, it was his hat. If it wasn't his hat, it was his socks. If it wasn't his clothing, it was his homework. One day, the boy wrote a list: "Pants and shirt are on the chair. Shoes and socks are beside the bed. My homework is in the school bag, and my bag is at the door." After a moment he added, "And I am in bed." The next morning he awoke to find everything exactly where the list indicated it would be, but he still came late to school. Try as he might, he could not find himself in bed.

This child is us. We are on a constant lookout for gadgets that remind us where we are. A friend recently told me about his new cell phone, with a GPS chip. "Now," he proudly said, "I can never get lost. My phone will always guide me back home."

A TIMELESS QUESTION

I caught myself reflecting on the first conversation that G-d had with man. Adam and Eve ate of the forbidden fruit, and G-d descended to investigate. Hearing Him approach, Adam went into hiding. "*Ayekah*?" called G-d. "Adam, where are you?"[1] G-d surely knew where Adam was, but he wanted Adam to know it too. Adam had sinned and G-d called him on it. "You have only been alive for ten hours,[2] and you have already defied My Will? What's going on with you?" asked G-d. "Where are you?"[3]

---

[1] Genesis 3:9.

[2] See *Babylonian Talmud, Sanhedrin* 38b.

[3] This interpretation is attributed to Reb Schneur Zalman of Liadi, the first Lubavitcher Rebbe. Rashi offered a simpler explanation. G-d knew that Adam was tense and sought to calm him with a conversation opener. Beit Rebbe, ch. 22.

This kind of question cannot be answered with a GPS signal. Because this is not so much a question of "Where are you?" but of "Who are you?"

THE IDENTITY QUESTION

We live in an ambiguous age and we often find it difficult to identify our true self. We must decide who and what we really are. At our very core, in our heart of hearts, at our point of quintessence, who are we? Am I a professional or a family member, a husband or a friend, a patriot or a Jew? What is my main role? What is in the forefront? What describes the true me?

We, in the Diaspora, live among host cultures that are larger than our own, and dominant. We often dress like them, act like them, and talk like them. We often befriend them, join their social circles, and identify with them.

The question, *"Ayekah?"* echoes through the corridors of time. It pierces the veil of history. Its unceasing demand prompts us to take a stand. We need to prioritize between the many hats that we wear, and choose from the many values that we juggle. What are my primary concerns? Are my secular studies more important than my Torah studies? Is acceptance in the right social circle more important than belonging to the Jewish nation? Is my commitment to my host nation greater than my commitment to Torah?

WHAT TO DO?

Imagine your child has auditioned for a theater troupe and landed a coveted role. She rehearses and practices. She's a wonderful actress. One day, you glance at the calendar and discover that the performance is scheduled for Saturday afternoon. What do you do? Does she perform? She has worked so hard. Does she stay at home? She will be devastated, not to mention that she will never be offered a central role again. What to do?

It is not so much a question of "What should we do?" but of "Who should we be?" Are we Jews who perform in the theater, or are we actors who practice Judaism? Which is uppermost? Which is primary? To be a good Jew or to fit in and succeed?

THE SEDER NIGHT

A Jewish high school basketball team surprised the league, and themselves, one year and made it to the semifinals. When they consulted the playoff schedule, they realized that one of the games was to be held on the first night of Passover. The players didn't even discuss the matter among themselves. It wasn't a question. Not a single player made an appearance that night. They were all at home, celebrating Passover with their families. That night, at the Seder table, they weren't basketball players who were Jewish, they were Jews who played basketball. They forfeited the game and lost their playoff berth. But with that loss, they confirmed their identity. That Seder night was not a loss. It was a victory.

ARE WE LIKE JOSEPH?

When Jacob's sons sold their brother Joseph to the Egyptians, he was a young lad who looked and acted like a Jew. When they met him again, twenty-two years later, they didn't recognize him. He was full-grown, and every bit the Egyptian prince. He dressed, behaved, talked, and walked like a prototype of Egyptian culture.[4] This wasn't the young Jewish lad they had last seen at home. This wasn't Joseph. This was an Egyptian prince. Little did they know that what they saw was just a facade, that on the inside Joseph was an utterly devout and passionately committed Jew. His dress belied his inner nature. His manner obscured his true identity. The brothers had no way of knowing this. To them, he was an Egyptian.

Like Joseph, we too must ensure that our Diaspora accoutrements do not affect our Jewish identity. Our Jewish "GPS signal" must ring with clarity, as we continually ask ourselves the timeless question, *"Ayeka?"* Are we keeping faith with the Jewish spark that we carry within?

The answer to this question will be accurate only when the question rings constantly in our heart. Then our heart will tell us that it isn't enough to identify culturally as a Jew. Cultures vary from one location to another and from one generation to the next. The only thread that

---

[4] *Genesis* 42:8. See Likutei Sichot, vol. III, p. 832

REACHING FOR G-D

truly binds all Jews, of all times and in all places, is Torah. This is what preserves our identity even in the Diaspora.

"How do we resolve our conflict of identity as Jews on the one hand, and loyal citizens to our host nation in the Diaspora, on the other?"

JEWISH LEADERS
NATIONAL PRIDE
Nearly two thousand years ago, the Jewish nation had its pride. I'm not talking about religious pride. I'm talking about national pride.

Yes, there was a time when we were a sovereign and powerful nation. We did what was right for Jews and didn't worry much about world opinion. We believed deeply, as deeply as humans can believe, that we had a right to self-governance and that, in a Jewish country, Jewish interests are the highest priority.

Ah, the nostalgia of long-forgotten times. Alas, those days are no more. Today we live in fear, even in our own country. What will others think? What might stimulate a wave of anti-Semitism? What might provoke the wrath of the Nations?[1]

A long and torturous Exile has left its mark on our suffering psyche. We bear this mark with pride, but it's a mark we would rather not bear at all.

CONFLICTED LOYALTIES
It is in this context that we wonder about which course Jews in the Diaspora should take when they discuss or get involved in their host country's politics. Should we rigorously defend Jewish causes, or should we absent ourselves from the debate? Should Jews who are elected to positions of power in non-Jewish countries bend over backwards to avoid creating an impression that we care more for our people than for our host country? Should we be Israel's silent ally or fierce friend?

---

[1] There are some ten members in the Israeli Knesset who represent Israeli Arabs. These members unabashedly champion Palestinian causes, to the detriment of the state they represent. They are not conflicted about this and harbor no fear of reprisals. They greet objections with utter surprise. "We are Arabs," they say. "What did you expect?"

VICEROY OF EGYPT

Let's take a page from Joseph's book. Joseph was a Jew. What's worse, he was a foreigner. Many countries pass laws against the appointment or election of a foreigner to positions of power. Yet Joseph was appointed viceroy of Egypt.[2]

His position was no doubt precarious. His every move was surely scrutinized. His every decision was surely critiqued. How did Joseph win the hearts and minds of the Egyptian people? By demonstrating his loyalty to Egyptian concerns.

FIRM, BUT LOVING

Joseph was appointed viceroy of Egypt, not ambassador of his Jewish family. When issues arose that affected the entire region, including his family, Joseph looked after the interests of Egypt first. But he never abandoned his family. Joseph foresaw a famine, and gathered provisions to provide for Egyptian citizens. He never asked Egyptians to provide for his family in Canaan. On the contrary, he sold food to non-Egyptians for exorbitant sums. These sums were deposited in Egyptian coffers. But when his own brothers arrived, he provided for them from his own coffers, not from the country's treasury.[3]

Joseph perceived that opening the borders to travelers from across the region exposed Egypt to unsavory characters who could enter the country for nefarious reasons, under the guise of obtaining provisions for their families. When Joseph's brothers arrived, they were clandestinely followed, interrogated, and incarcerated on charges of espionage. In their case, it was only a ruse,

---

[2] *Genesis* 41:39–46.

[3] *Genesis* 41:33–36; ibid. 56–57. See also *Genesis* 43:44–45. It was only when Pharaoh ordered that Joseph's family be fed from Egypt's coffers that Joseph agreed to do so. (*Genesis* 45:17–21 and 45:5–6.)

but the episode suggests that Joseph had established a bureau of counterespionage to secure the safety of his country.[4]

When Egyptian citizens depleted their stores, Joseph provided for them from the country's treasury. When they could no longer afford to purchase food from the treasury, Joseph instituted a policy of social welfare and provided food free of charge.[5]

Joseph's integrity, transparency, and industrious commitment won over the hearts of the citizenry. They trusted their Jewish viceroy, because he put their interests first. Yet Joseph never forgot his family.

The plight of his family always concerned him, and he reached out to help them. Because of his position, he was always careful to align his family's interests with those of Egypt. He invited his family to Egypt and provided for them, but he made certain that Pharaoh and the citizens understood that hosting his family would also benefit Egypt. He explained that the presence of pious people would protect Egypt and deliver blessing to the country.[6] Indeed, the famine in Egypt lifted on the day that Jacob arrived.[7]

TO BE LIKE JOSEPH

Joseph's shining example must serve as a guidepost to our generation. Jews who are citizens in non-Jewish countries, especially Jews elected or appointed to positions of leadership in such countries, must demonstrate loyalty to their respective countries. However, looking after their country's interests does not absolve them from obligations to their own people.

Regardless of citizenship, we must remain loyal to our People. We must not look on with equanimity when our country's interests conflict with those of our People. We must make the strongest effort to reconcile the differences between the two causes. Like Joseph in days of old, we too must respond.

---

[4] *Genesis* 42:1–20.

[5] *Genesis* 47:13–26.

[6] *Midrash Tanchuma*, Naso, ch. 26.

[7] *Tosefta* 10:3. It is also noteworthy that the famine returned after Jacob's passing.

When Jews are in distress, Jewish politicians must seek and vigorously adopt solutions that serve the interest of their People and their country.

This nuanced path could grow complicated. Advocating such solutions could provoke anti-Semitic allegations. But with trust in G-d, faith in the righteousness of our cause, and a transparent display of loyalty to our host countries, Jews in the Diaspora and even Jewish politicians can thrive and succeed.

Reaching for extremes is the easy way out; Joseph's balance is the true challenge. Do we have the courage to be like Joseph?

"We have discussed trust in G-d, serving G-d, and obedience to G-d. I realize that one more ingredient is necessary to complete the picture: love for G-d. What can you tell me about love for G-d?"

LIVING FOR G-D

THREE LOVES

"And you shall love G-d your Lord with all your heart, with all your soul, and with all your might."[1] These words are not poetic descriptions of love. They are precise instructions that define the parameters of the love that G-d requires from us.

According to our Sages, the words "with all your heart" teach us that our primary desire for G-d must subordinate all our other desires. The words "with all your soul" instruct us to love G-d more than we love our very lives. We must love Him with every fiber of our being, irrespective of any sacrifice this love may entail. In short, we must stand prepared even to die for G-d.

The words "with all your might" instruct us to love G-d with all our resources. Every possession must be devoted to His service. We must be prepared to devote our last penny to His cause. An alternative interpretation of "with all your might" is to love G-d in all circumstances that Providence assigns us. We must love him in bliss and in distress, in joy and in misfortune. In other words, we must be prepared not only to die for G-d, but also to live for Gd.[2]

LIVING AND DYING

The sequence of the first two clauses is clearly structured in order of ascent. It is easier to desire G-d with our hearts than it is to love him with our lives.

---

[1] *Deuteronomy* 6:5.

[2] *Babylonian Talmud, Brachot* 61b.

But the placement of the third clause seems curious. Having been instructed to die for G-d, is it necessary that we be instructed to live for him?[3]

The answer is yes. Because, though dying for G-d is heroic, the ultimate sacrifice and the pinnacle of devotion, it is not a *constant* sacrifice. It is a sacrifice that lasts for but a moment. Living our life in accordance with G-d's wishes, even when such devotion engenders great and constant sacrifice, is a lasting indication of enduring love.

Further analysis of the three clauses will yield a better understanding of the three loves, and of why living for G-d requires a deeper love than dying for G-d.

Husband and Wife

The love between a Jew and G-d is compared to the love between husband and wife. Reflecting on marital love may help us distinguish between the three standards of love: heartfelt love, dying for love, and living for love.

Let's consider newlyweds. They feel heartfelt love for each other. Their primary desire is for each other; all other desires are subordinate to this one. They truly love each other. But they are not prepared to die for each other. Jumping in front of a train to save a loved one requires a higher level of devotion than heartfelt love. Heartfelt love means that we enjoy living with our loved one. Dying for the one we love means that life without our loved one is not worth living. "I love you," does not imply such devotion. It implies only that I love living with you. But if I tragically lost you, I would sadly learn to live without you.

A husband and wife who are prepared die for each other have established a profound bond; their devotion to each other is exemplary. But it is not yet a

---

[3] The Talmudic response to this question seems at first glance even more curious than the question itself. "Yes," says the Talmud, "There are indeed people who value their possessions ahead of their lives." Does the Torah ascribe such shallow motives to pious lovers of G-d? This essay reveals a deeper meaning to the Talmudic response.

bond of the highest magnitude. That distinction is reserved for the couple who is not only prepared to die for each other, but is also prepared to live for each other.

Now let's consider a husband who discovers, to his great misfortune, that his wife has contracted a severe disease. She has become bedridden and will require constant care. Their hopes and dreams are shattered: They will never have children. They will never travel together. They will never experience the life that they envisioned. He must now alter his life completely and become a permanent caregiver. The husband who stands by his wife in such circumstances has reached the deepest level of love.[4] Living with this daily and hourly sacrifice, for years or even decades, is far more difficult than making the ultimate sacrifice in a split-second decision. The latter is the ultimate sacrifice. But the former is the more enduring sacrifice.[5]

ON A DEEPER LEVEL

Living for a loved one is purely selfless, but dying for a loved one is not. A husband dies for his wife because he cannot conceive of living without her. It is true that his primary concern is for her safety, but he is also subtly influenced by the desperate thought that life without her is not worth living. Living for a loved one is purely selfless. The husband would gain much if he abandoned his wife in her hour of need and pursued his own life selfishly and unencumbered. He stands by her only because he loves her. His devotion is pure and selfless; it serves only the one he loves.

---

[4] This is not a reflection on the value of life. The sacrifice of life is the ultimate sacrifice; no other is comparable to it. A moment of life is of absolute value, while decades of loneliness and grief are of subjective value. This is a reflection on the motivation that drives the sacrifice. An enduring sacrifice requires greater motivation than a sacrifice resulting from a split-second decision.

[5] Consider a mother and father who watch their child wander into the path of an oncoming train. They have only a moment to decide who will die to save the child and who will live to raise him. Which is the more difficult decision? The parent who dies will suffer for a moment. The parent who lives will suffer for years.

We now return to our love for G-d. The three levels of love commanded in the Torah are indeed in order of ascent. First we must learn to love G-d with all our heart, ensuring that our primary desire for G-d subordinates all other desires. We then gradually grow to love G-d with all our soul, standing prepared, if necessary, to die for G-d. The third and deepest level of love is the one that impels us to live all our life for G-d.

PRACTICAL EXPRESSION

Living for G-d is the highest level of love, yet its expression is through everyday actions. It is not reserved for the deeply pious or celebrated Torah scholars; it is within easy reach of every Jew. Every time we "sacrifice" a moment of our time to perform a mitzvah, every time we subordinate our possessions to G-d's service, every time we forgo worldly pleasure for an hour of Torah study, we demonstrate absolute devotion that flows from the greatest level of love known to man.

Love is most potent when it is translated into action.

"Before I can love my wife, I must first find her. How can I find the match that is destined for me by G-d?"

THE MATCHMAKER
A MODERN COURTSHIP

The first discussion of courtship and marriage in the Torah is the story of Isaac and Rebecca. Far from today's typical vision of romance, their story begins with Abraham dispatching his servant Eliezer to find a wife for his son Isaac.

Had they met in the modern age, their courtship might have looked like this: While each dreaming of meeting the right person, their paths would one day cross. Isaac would notice Rebecca and catch her interest with a surreptitious glance. Rebecca would briefly acknowledge his glance, and then quickly turn away. The brief encounter would leave them both wondering.

Isaac would ask Rebecca on a date and she, secretly thrilled, but not wanting to appear overly eager, would casually accept. Over dinner, they would strike an interested but cautious pose; each worried that their strong feelings might not be mutual. One date would lead to another, each the product of much planning and anxiety, until eventually they would become an official "couple." They would talk, dine, and enjoy each other's company, but the question of marriage would be left unexamined. The uncomfortable uncertainty about the future, about the other's long-term intentions, would go on for a while. Each would wonder what the other was thinking, but be afraid to ask. Finally, one of them would gather the courage and bring up the fateful question.

A SHIDDUCH

Isaac and Rebecca were spared this agony. Abraham treated them to a *shidduch*, an arranged marriage. Abraham commissioned his servant *Eliezer* to find a match for Isaac. *Eliezer* found Rebecca and introduced her to Isaac. The couple met briefly and were married on the same day. Did they love each other on their wedding day? They barely knew each other. The love and admiration would come later.[1] Unexciting? Unromantic? Maybe. But let's take a closer look at the *shidduch* system.

In a *shidduch* situation, young men and women also date. They also spend time together and get to know each other well. However, the process begins in a very different way. It begins when young men and women consult with a matchmaker. A skilled matchmaker must have wisdom and intuition. The job of the matchmaker is to identify the needs, character, goals, and outlook of each individual and propose an appropriate match.

This initial step of consulting a matchmaker saves young men and women much anguish. They avoid the emotionally hazardous process of blind dating and the frightening prospect of discovering, only after they are deeply involved, that they have little in common with each other. The matchmaker ensures that they meet only those with whom they share at least some essential goals and outlooks. Thus they are prepared to meet for the first time and realistically explore whether they are right for each other.

The purpose of the first date, fairly casual yet focused, is to identify common interests and values. Aware that both are seeking, and ready for, the commitment of marriage, they are clear about the purpose of their meetings. This lends vitality to the courtship. Knowing that marriage to this person could be imminent, the usual hesitation about disclosing personal information is overcome. They welcome honest discussion, ask direct questions to help discover each other's true character, and subtly, but no less importantly, take note of the chemistry between them.

Subsequent dates strike a more serious tone, turning from their present to their future. Subjects such as family, struggles and ambitions, specific goals and aspirations are broached with relative ease. Each person describes the life he or she hopes to lead. If they share a common vision and an attraction to each other, then they have a foundation on which a marriage can be built.

---

[1] *Genesis* 24. See also Rashi on 24:67.

If either feels that they are incompatible, they simply discontinue the courtship. Sometimes the decision to separate can be difficult emotionally, since they may have invested much. Yet the entire process is conducted with mutual respect, in privacy, and with dignity.

A GATEWAY

In the *shidduch* system, the match is indeed not the product of fiery romance. On their wedding day, bride and groom are joyous, content with their current mutual admiration, respect, and commitment. As long as they share the same values and are both deeply committed to the marriage, they know they can overcome any obstacles and resolve any differences that may lie ahead. They know that true love takes decades for anyone to build.

On their wedding day, along with their relationship of the moment, bride and groom are focused on the decades to come. They view this day as a foundation on which they will build and develop their love and their life together. Their marriage is rooted in respect and admiration, strengthened by devotion and commitment, and laced with happiness and growing love. Such a marriage is a tribute to G-d. Such was the marriage between our Patriarch Isaac and our Matriarch Rebecca.

May all marriages be so blessed.

"Do you have any further insights about marriage?"

THE DANCING JEW
THE HORA
I'm not much of a dancer, so I often find myself on the sidelines of the dance floor, watching rather than joining. The dance pace at a Chassidic wedding is intense, but the selection is pretty much standard: the hora, the hora, and yet another version of the hora. Actually, when you think of it, the hora is symbolic of marriage: Dancers join hands, and dance in a tight circle, symbolizing the closeness and emotional intimacy that the couple hopes to achieve.[1]

AN INSPIRED DANCE
The hora is indeed a beautiful dance, but I was once at a wedding where a much more inspired dance was performed. The dance floor was filled with circles, various styles of the hora. Then two young Chassidim squared off and began an intricate and soulful "inspired dance," as I call it.[2] The dance floor emptied as everyone gathered to enjoy the spectacle. The dancers faced off at a distance and acknowledged each other with a curt bow. The dance began slowly, as they circled each other, turning toward and away from each other. Animatedly, they angled back and forth, alternating between drawing closer and pulling away.

To me, the choreographed steps told an exquisite tale of two people who yearned for closeness with each other, and were too hesitant to reach out. The dancers slowly drew near, in their yearning, but then quickly reversed themselves and pulled away. They drew closer again, only to pull back once more, and gaze at each other from a distance.

---

[1] The circle represents perfect equality, since it has no beginning or end, no head or tail, no top or bottom.

[2] Ironically "Broigez tantz"- angry dance, is its real name; it's about two friends who are angry with each other, and trying to reconcile.

As the dance progressed so did the pace, and the dancers wound their way across the floor. They advanced and fell back, each time drawing progressively closer. They twisted and turned, barely avoiding, nearly colliding in their quest for mutual closeness. The dance wound to an end, the dancers warmly embraced. The spectators applauded, celebrating the triumph of peace, love, and happiness.

SIBLINGS AND SPOUSES

The drama that played itself out on the floor reflects the journey of married life. Marriage requires enthusiasm, commitment, and love, but above all, diligent and constant care. It is a never-ending process of drawing together and a never-ending challenge of overcoming obstacles. After all, man and woman are opposite in nature and character; marriage brings together two diametric opposites. Loving unity between spouses is dynamic; it thrives on being in a constant state of flux. It grows and fades, only to grow back again, even stronger than before. Like that "inspired dance," it rises and falls, peaks and dips, advances and retreats.

The hora, on the other hand, maintains a close, steady pace, with no surprises, and very little drama. There is no fanfare and no triumph, symbolic more of the relationship between siblings than that of husband and wife. Siblings play out their own little dance, natural and easy. They are from the same family; they share common traits, background, attitudes. Their bond is innate, lifelong and unbreakable. By contrast, married couples must work hard to forge their bond. And even after this is achieved, there's no guarantee of permanence. Marriages can explode in rage or fade away in cold apathy, dying in divorce.

The "inspired dance" is artistic and dramatic; the hora is natural and predictable. The question we must ask is: With whom shall we dance the hora and with whom the inspired dance? This is also the question we ask as Jews. Which of these two do we "dance" with G-d?

THE JEW AND G-D

The proper answer is: both. G-d and humans are as distant from each other as finiteness from infinity. He is the Creator and we are merely the created.

In this sense, our dance before Him is the inspired dance; we reach across this gulf, yearning and struggling to forge and maintain a connection. Yet, at the same time, G-d's bond with us pierces the core of our essence. Even the totally assimilated Jew, even the apostate, cannot cease being a Jew. On the deepest level, we are claimed by G-d. Like a sibling, who cannot sue for divorce, our dance is the hora. We are forever together, in an eternal circle that joins us in its fold.

The Torah calls the Jewish People the bride of G-d. But beautiful as this term is, it doesn't promise eternal connection. The bond of bride and groom is loving, and hopefully eternal. But not necessarily. Tragically, some marriages end in divorce.

However, the Torah also calls Jews G-d's sister. Our sibling relationship with G-d is immutable and enduring; it can never be severed. Every Jew is a sister and a bride. We, the accomplished dancers, are proficient in the intricate steps of both dances — the hora and the inspired dance.[3]

TWO SOULS

This bride/sister duality, dancing our dual dance with G-d, is the role of every Jew. G-d granted the Jew a G-dly soul and an animal soul. The G-dly soul is a veritable part of G-d, clothed in the garment of the human body. As we walk, think, and talk, we carry a fragment of our Creator within our person. It is the essence of who we are; we can neither surrender it nor divorce it. The animal soul is the conventional soul of man, which exists to a lesser degree in all living organisms. The animal soul feels no natural kinship with its Creator. It is not inherently holy. On the contrary, its primal attraction is to that which is earthly.

If it is ever to develop a relationship with G-d, this animal soul must be slowly nurtured, with loving care. Given the correct dynamics, our animal soul can learn to connect with G-d, but its connection cannot be spontaneous or permanent. While connected, it will be fiercely drawn to G-dliness. It will

---

[3] "I have come to my garden, my sister the bride" (Shir Hashirim 5:1).

covet all things holy and enjoy a spectacularly rousing love, but this connection is by no means assured. It can fade as quickly as it rises. It requires constant tending.

Our animal soul is (or has the potential to be) G-d's bride. The bride prefers the inspired dance, where a powerful connection is possible, though it requires constant effort and emotional investment. Our G-dly soul is "G-d's sister"; the sister prefers the hora, always connected, always dependable. Some Jews are more devout, some are more impassioned, but no Jew is more connected to G-d than another. The G-dly soul of even the most assimilated Jew remains eternally linked with G-d. Even after long separations, G-d and His siblings connect with familiarity and ease. [4]

No matter where we roam, G-d's House is still our home.

---

[4] The cosmos plays out the same dance, but plays it across the broader horizon of the sky. The sun rises every morning and sets every night, offering bright rays of light and an enveloping blanket of warmth. It is dependable and permanent. It dances a daily hora around the universe. The moon, by contrast, also winds its way about the global dance floor, but it appears to wax and wane, to be dynamic rather than static, seeming continuously to adjust its appearance. It is not today what it was yesterday; it will not be tomorrow what it is today. It can be depended upon to do only one thing, to grow or shrink. It prefers the inspired dance rather than the hora. This essay is based on *Zohar*, vol. 3, p. 89a, and on Ohr Ha-torah, *Leviticus*, vol. 1, p. 578.

"Why did G-d create the gulf between us and Him? Wouldn't it be better if our relationship were smooth and dependable? What do we gain from the gulf?"

THE DEEPER BOND

OPPOSITES

Opposites attract. Some say this is because life with a like-minded spouse would be too agreeable, and therefore boring. I say, really? I know many couples who would welcome such boredom. Life with a like-minded spouse is smooth and efficient. There is no wasted energy on quarrels and disagreements, no major arguments about minor issues. Opposites seem to disagree about everything: when to vacation, where to eat, how much money to spend ... They yearn to make things simple, but they just can't agree. Yet, the fact is that, despite their disagreements, most quarrelsome couples remain committed to each other. This is one of the world's many wonders. Why is this so? What is the secret of their commitment?

Marriage. Marriage means commitment. Not a commitment to a working marriage, but a commitment to make marriage work. Couples betrothed, form a bond in the depth of their souls. Beyond the pleasure of each other's company, beyond their passion for each other, lies a love that cannot be described.

BECOMING ONE

In marriage, a part of you in invested in your spouse. You cannot tear away from your spouse without tearing away from yourself. Marriage creates a new entity that didn't exist before, composed of both spouses. Thinking of life without your spouse becomes inconceivable. Once married, you're no longer compatible with yourself unless you're compatible with your spouse. That's what marriage does. It fuses husband and wife till they become one. That's why quarreling couples stay in their relationship. Their bond far exceeds their differences. This is also why opposites attract.

Life with an agreeable spouse is smooth, placid, but it doesn't stimulate the profound marital bond that a marriage of opposites does. The couple that is not challenged to prove their commitment to each other and arouse their deep and abiding love, simply don't; they cruise along "on automatic" till they run into an obstacle. It is one of our failings as humans that we don't grow unless provoked; we draw on inner resources only when obstacles are placed before us, only when we are forced to clamber over hurdles. Life with an opposite spouse presents one hurdle after another; it may be challenging, but it's a challenge that evokes resilience. They may constantly have differences of opinion, but in the heat of their spirited discussions, their true bond is forged. Such marriages are complex, but they are deeper and richer, too.

SUPERNAL MARRIAGE

The relationship between husband and wife mirrors the relationship between ourselves and G-d. At Sinai, G-d entered into a covenant with our people. He pledged to love and provide for us. We pledged to love and obey Him. The relationship has survived thousands of years, though it can hardly be labeled smooth. At times, we are close to Him; at times, distant. At times, we are fervent in our love; at times, angry. This works both ways. G-d turns from us and allows us to suffer; we turn from G-d and allow Him to wait for us in vain.

Why did G-d make it so? Had He attuned us to the beauty of Torah, our relationship would have been mutually agreeable and delightful. Why did He close our eyes to the delights of Divinity, but open them to selfish and physical pleasures?

Because He wanted us to be challenged. When we are tempted by that which lures us away from Him, we're forced to ask ourselves deep and penetrating questions: Who are we? Why are we here? Why should we be dedicated to our relationship with G-d? What is unique about our People?

The perfectly pious and wholly devout are not conflicted; they are content in their relationship with G-d; they don't torment themselves with such existential questions. This is the easier course, but it is not as rewarding. Because questions that are never asked remain forever unanswered. A course strewn with pitfalls precipitates a storm of questions. The questions demand answers, and the answers evoke our love for G-d. Our relationship is more complex this way, but it is richer and deeper, too.

THE "NOW" ERA
We can now understand the deeper meaning of a curious phrase that Moses used when he addressed the Israelites. He said, "Now, Israel, what does G-d your Lord ask of you, but to fear ... and to love Him?"[1]

Why did Moses preface the question with the word, "now"? Also, why did he phrase the statement as a [rhetorical] question, when he could simply have stated G-d's wish?

Moses addressed the people as Israelites, a name they received after their forefather Jacob quarreled with and triumphed over Esau's angel. The Hebrew name "Yisrael," comes from the Hebrew word "sarita," which means "you have struggled with." Indeed, we each struggle with our virtual Esau, our little inner voice that lures us from G-d's Torah and steers us toward coarse and selfish pleasures. This struggle is made possible by G-d concealing Himself, denying us the ability to see His true beauty. If we could truly perceive Divine beauty, material pleasures wouldn't tempt us. In fact, in the Messianic era, we will no longer crave material indulgence, because G-d will then lift the veil, and His true beauty will be perceived by all.

Moses opened with the word, "now" because this struggle, the struggle of "Yisrael," takes place only now, in the current era, in contradistinction to the future, Messianic, era, when there will be no struggle at all.[2]

THE INNER "WHAT"
Why does G-d make it so that we have to struggle? He wants us to stimulate our "what." What is our what? It is the inner core of our soul, that recognizes G-d as the Only true Entity of meaning. By comparison, every other meaning

---

[1] *Deuteronomy* 10:12.

[2] For a similar, but slightly different, slant on the word "what," see Ohr HaChayim, ibid.

is negated. They are nothing but *what*? This negation need not be stated. It is sufficient to imply it in a one-word rhetorical question.

Moses said of Aaron and of himself, "What are we?" He wasn't asking a question so much as making a statement: We are nothing but *what*? A rhetorical question, diminished by any attempt at response.[3]

The Talmud teaches, "Who is a fool? Those who lose what they are given."[4] When the Talmud speaks of fools, it is referring to sinners, as evidenced in the Talmudic dictum, "All sinners are overcome by a spirit of folly, that prompts them to forget their bond with G-d."[5]

Who is a fool? Another way of asking the same question is, "Who is a sinner?" Those who lose the innate sense of *"what"* that they were given. In other words, those who reject their souls and their core acceptance of G-d.[6]

Without the struggle, it is nearly impossible to experience the inner core, the *"what."* This is why G-d forced us into a quarrelsome relationship with Him, where we must struggle with our personal Esau, overcome it, and earn the name Israel. It is the only way to uncover our core and experience our *"what."*

Let's go back and reread the verse. "Now, Israel, what does G-d your Lord ask of you, but to fear ... and to love Him?" It is a question. Why did G-d ordain the struggle of "Israel" in this era of "now"? Because, "What, does G-d,

---

[3] *Exodus* 16:7.

[4] *Babylonian Talmud, Chagigah* 4a.

[5] *Babylonian Talmud, Sotah* 3a.

[6] This is also why our Sages said, "An Israelite, even though he sins is still an Israelite" (*Babylonian Talmud, Sanhedrin* 44a). They didn't speak of a Jew, but of an Israelite. Israelites are those who struggle against their inner Esau. Even when Israelites act like fools by losing the *what* that they are given and allowing themselves to be overcome by the spirit of folly, they remain, at heart and in essence, Israelites — people who have the inner strength to overcome their inclinations and to repent.

Your Lord want from you." He wants us to stimulate our *"what,"* which leads to a life of passionate emotion that allows us to "fear and love Him."[7]

A relationship of struggle is not easy, but if dealt with correctly, its liabilities can become assets. This is true in marriage, and it is certainly true in Judaism. When wrestling with our own weaknesses, we are forced to explore our reasons for struggling. The more we ask a question, the sharper the answer becomes.

---

[7] This essay is based in part on Ohr Hatorah, *Devarim,* p. 678 and Sefer Mamaarim Melukat, vol. II, p. 325.

Part Four — Miscellaneous Questions

"What does Jewish tradition have to say about the Jewish woman?"

The Proud Jewish Mother
Forever

She was there at the very beginning, and she is there for us still now. She was there in times of elation and was there in times of distress. She was there in times of hope and is still there in times of despair. She nurtured our faith under the Inquisition and our strength during the pogroms. She held our hands in the gas chambers and holds our hands still. She is our Yiddishe Mama — the Jewish Mother.

The Matriarchs

I wasn't there when Ishmael threatened to take Isaac's life, but if I had been, I don't think I could have stood up to him with the same determination that Sarah did.[1] I wasn't there when Isaac proposed to bestow his blessing on Esau, but if I had been, I doubt that I could have found the courage to do what Rebecca did and send in Jacob as a substitute.[2]

Rachel selflessly forfeited her sacred right to be interred beside her husband in the Cave of Patriarchs and Matriarchs. She chose to be buried in Bethlehem, for the sake of her children. When, more than a thousand years later, the Temple in Jerusalem was destroyed and our ancestors were exiled to

---

[1] *Tosefta, Sotah* 6. See also Rashi on *Genesis* 21:9–10. Ishmael taunted Isaac about the inheritance, claiming that as firstborn he, Ishamael, was entitled to a double portion. When Isaac balked at a concubine's son claiming the birthrights Ishmael shot arrows his way. Our Sages taught that Ishmael engaged in murder, idolatry, and adultery. Sarah hastened to remove this negative influence from her son, Isaac.

[2] *Genesis* 27:1–15. Rebecca risked not only her physical safety, but also her spiritual safety. When Jacob worried that Isaac might discover his duplicity, and give him a curse instead of a blessing, Rebecca assured Jacob that the curse would be on *her* head (*Genesis* 28:13).

REACHING FOR G-D

Babylon, they passed through Bethlehem and paused at their Mother Rachel's Tomb to pray. Rachel, who had waited for this moment for centuries, stormed the Gates of Heaven and shed bitter tears. G-d granted her wish and promised that the Exile would end after seventy years. If not for Rachel, the Babylonian Exile might not have ended so quickly; our nation might not have survived.[3]

Throughout our history, every time a need has arisen, it was the Jewish mothers who responded.

Sarah didn't worry about standing up to the violent Ishmael; her son's safety was at stake. Had Ishmael accomplished then what his descendants have tried to accomplish ever since, our people would not be here today. Rebecca didn't fear Esau's wrath; her children's future was at stake. Had Jacob not received those blessings, there might not have been a Jewish People today. Rachel's children were in need, and she never wavered. She worried not for herself, but for her children.[4]

IN EGYPT

Pharaoh decreed that all Jewish male newborns be put to death. Hearing this, Jewish men despaired and refused to procreate, but their wives wouldn't hear of this. They took action, because the future of their People was at stake. Contrary to their modest natures, they ventured out to the

---

[3] Rashi on *Genesis* 28:7. Though Rashi suggests that Jacob buried her there according to Divine instruction, and that Rachel didn't express an opinion on this, see Likutei Sichot XXX, p. 238, that Rachel demanded this as well. See also *Bereishit Rabbah* 82:10. For the general description of this story see *Jeremiah* 31:14–16 and *Pesichta D'eicha Rabti* 24.

[4] Rachel was meant to marry Jacob, but her father put Leah under the wedding canopy instead. Rachel and Jacob had arranged a private code to protect themselves against precisely such duplicity, but Rachel, at the last moment, surrendered this code to her sister. (*Megillah* 13b) Rachel also hid under the marital bed and made all the proper sounds in Leah's stead, so that Jacob wouldn't discover the ruse and shame her sister. She turned the night of her dreams into her worst nightmare, all to protect her sister from embarrassment. (*Pesichta D'eicha Rabti* 24)

fields and enticed their working husbands. When they felt the pangs of labor, they returned to the fields, far from prying eyes, to give birth. They then returned home, entrusting their infants' survival to G-d. G-d nurtured these children lovingly and, when they matured, brought them home.[5]

To ensure the success of his decree against the Jewish children, Pharaoh instructed Jewish midwives to commit infanticide. But, the midwives never entertained the idea; they saved countless lives, at grave personal risk.[6] Still, despite their efforts, Egyptian soldiers sought out the children and cast them into the Nile.

In the face of this cruel decree, *Amram* divorced his wife, *Yocheved*. But their six-year-old daughter, *Miriam*, argued that Pharaoh's decree threatened only the male newborns, while divorce ensured the complete extinction of the Jewish nation. So *Amram* and *Yocheved* remarried. When their son Moses was born, it was *Miriam*, who gave the people new hope, when she prophesied that the baby would grow up to become the redeemer of Israel.[7]

Imagine Yocheved's anguish as she placed her son in a basket and cast him onto the Nile, entrusting his safety to G-d. Imagine *Miriam's* dread as she watched none other than Pharaoh's daughter, the princess of Egypt, collect the basket. Imagine her courage as she approached the princess and audaciously recommended her mother, *Yocheved*, as a wet nurse for the baby.[8]

Batya was the princess who stretched out her arm to collect the little Jewish boy. Our Sages taught that she had ventured out to the river to secretly immerse, as the final step in her conversion to Judaism. Imagine her bravery,

---

[5] They believed with perfect faith that G-d would not abandon them. G-d had promised Jacob that his children would be redeemed from Egypt, and the Jewish mothers fought to give G-d that chance. See Rashi on *Exodus* 38:8 and *Shemot Rabbah* 23:8.

[6] *Exodus* 1:16–2.

[7] Rashi on *Exodus* 2:1. See *Babylonian Talmud, Sotah* 13a, and *Mechilta* on *Exodus* 15:20.

[8] *Exodus* 2:3–9.

returning to the palace, to the mighty Pharaoh's home, secretly collaborating with the Jews to raise their future redeemer, under her father's very nose. Self-sacrifice par excellence![9]

These are some of the famous stories of the greatness of Jewish mothers. But there are countless stories that are unknown to us, countless unsung heroines, throughout our history — Jewish mothers, who selflessly sacrificed for the sake of their children, with no regard to personal safety.[10] Jewish mothers taught their daughters to light Shabbat candles in Catholic Spain, despite the threat of death at the hands of the Inquisition. Jewish mothers in Nazi death camps who continued to bear children and who, with their last breath, defied

---

[9] *Babylonian Talmud, Sotah* 12b. That is why she was named *Batya*. Rather than *Bat Paro*, "daughter of Pharaoh," she became, on conversion, the "daughter of G-d."

[10] The list of Jewish mothers who stood by their people in times of need includes many heroines: *Esther*, who forfeited her marriage to *Mordechai* for the sake of saving her People (*Babylonian Talmud, Megillah* 13a, 13b, and 15a). *Tamar*, who was prepared to die at the stake rather than shame Judah, the father of her children (*Babylonian Talmud, Sotah* 10b. See also Rashi on *Genesis* 38:28). The daughters of *Lot*, who despite living in Sodom, that G-dless city, were chaste and moral women, as the Torah testifies (*Genesis* 19:8). When Sodom was destroyed, they thought that all of humanity had perished, except their immediate family. Despite their revulsion, they forced themselves into incest, in an effort to perpetuate humanity. (ibid., verses 31–38. See also *Bereshit Rabbah* 49:9) Ruth, who was modest by nature, acted brazenly in going to *Boaz*, because her mother-in-law, the righteous *Naomi* instructed her to do so. King David was the product of their union. (Ruth and *Boaz* did not actually have relations until they were properly married.) Ruth subjected herself to personal mortification and possible rejection by her benefactor, for the benefit of the Jewish People. (*Ruth* 3:1–15. See also *Crown of Creation*, p. 91.) Three generations later, *Nitzevet*, mother of King David acted in a similar way to bring him to the world (Sefer Hatoda'ah, introduction to *Shavuot*). *Channah*, mother of seven sons, urged her children to surrender their lives rather than worship idols. After they were executed, the distraught mother went mad, and fell from a roof to her tragic death. (*Babylonian Talmud, Gitin* 57b; *Eichah Rabbah* 1:50, where she appears by the name *Miriam Bat Nachtom*). These are but a few of many such examples.

the Final Solution. Jewish mothers under Communist oppression who raised their children to be proud Jews, despite Soviet discrimination and persecution.

What Is the Source of Their Strength?

The source of their strength is their faith. From the very beginning, Jewish women trusted in G-d, in a personal and caring G-d. Even when the men despaired, the women believed and carried on. When the future seemed bleak, when events seemed at their worst, the women never lost hope. They never broke faith. They always believed that G-d would come through. If not immediately, then soon. If not for them, then for their children.

When G-d split the Reed Sea, Miriam, accompanied by the joyous jangling of tambourines, led the women in an song of praise to G-d. Where did they find tambourines in the middle of a desert? They brought them along from Egypt, in perfect faith that G-d would perform just such miracles.[11] When Moses failed to return from Mount Sinai at the appointed time, and men predicted that he wouldn't come back, the women persisted in their faith. When the men decided to build a Golden Calf, the Jewish women refused to contribute their gold.[12] When the spies returned from the Holy Land with a negative report, the men broke down and cried. But the women never broke faith with G-d. They rejected the negative report and refused to cry.[13]

This ironclad faith is the source of the Jewish mother's rock-like strength. Faith is the cornerstone of our religion; it is our foundation. Our mothers give us that foundation, on which we build. Foundations are usually not visible. They are concealed by the buildings atop them, but in emergencies, when the building crumbles, the foundation can once again be glimpsed. It is rock solid and it cannot be shaken. The entire building can be rebuilt on it.

---

[11] *Mechilta* on Exodus 15:20.

[12] *Midrash* Tanchuma, Ki Tisa 19. See also *Bamidbar Rabbah* 21:10.

[13] *Bamidbar Rabbah* 21:10 and Rashi on *Numbers* 26:64.

WISE OF HEART

This is why the Torah identifies the women who helped to build the Tabernacle as "wise of heart." Wisdom of heart pertains to immutable faith and steadfast strength. Indeed, these were the builders of our Tabernacle. These were the true founders of our nation.[14]

Moses did his part. Aaron did his. The rabbis, judges, teachers, and priests all did their part. Master builders and gifted architects constructed the Tabernacle. But it would all have come to nothing if not for the contribution of those Jewish mothers who were "wise at heart." With their heart-wisdom, these women planted the seeds of faith that grew into a nation. With their heart-wisdom, these women produced generations of Jews who could face every trial with the fortitude of that rock-solid faith that is their heritage.

Jewish pride is not born in a vacuum; it was lovingly cultivated over many generations. The Jewish family unit is responsible for our powerful sense of identity; the Jewish mother is the chief architect of the family.

---

[14] *Exodus* 35:25. See also *Shemot Rabbah* 49:1. The Torah also refers to the men as wise of heart and inspired (*Exodus* 35:25 and 36:1–2), but the fact that the women are introduced before the men is unusual, requiring explanation. Furthermore, the Torah specifies that the women outdid the men in their contribution to the Tabernacle (*Exodus* 35:22).

"Yes, but the heroes and heroines of our past lived in an age far removed from our own, and with concerns far different than our own. How are they relevant to us today?"

TO THOSE WHO PAVED OUR WAY
MANY HELPING HANDS

Ben Zoma used to say, "How many labors Adam carried out before he obtained bread to eat! He plowed, sowed, reaped, bound, threshed, winnowed, and selected the grain. He ground, sifted, kneaded and baked, and then at last he ate. Whereas I arise, and find all these things done for me."[1]

In our generation of instant satisfaction, the art of gratitude is nearly lost. How often do we pause to consider the tailor who made the shirt we wear, the truck driver who delivered the goods we purchase at the store, and the countless hands that labor in the background to provide our many comforts? The farmer grows the wheat, the wholesaler sells, the distributor supplies, the baker bakes, and the salesperson sells the bread. If we consider them, their support staff, and all those who provide the products and ingredients, we realize how many people work together to produce a single dinner for us.

GRATITUDE FOR TORAH

If we must learn to be grateful to those who produce items that answer our physical needs, then we must surely learn to appreciate those who provide for our spiritual needs. In the Torah, we read that Moses rebuked our ancestors for not having served G-d with gladness and goodness of heart, when *"everything"* was abundant.[2] The Talmud teaches that the word *"everything"* refers to the Torah.[3] According to at least one commentator, Moses was chiding our ancestors because they were ungrateful for the gift of Torah.[4]

---

[1] *Babylonian Talmud, Brachos* 58a.

[2] *Deuteronomy* 28:47.

[3] *Babylonian Talmud, Nedarim* 41a.

[4] Commentary of Meshech Chochmoh on *Deuteronomy* 28:48.

When we fulfill the commandments of the Torah, we show appreciation not only for the Torah but also for the many generations that came before us, and were persecuted for their faith. They risked their lives to study Torah. They taught it, preserved its traditions and transmitted it to us. When we abandon the Torah, we betray them and their many sacrifices.

POINTS OF SACRIFICE

Our Patriarch Abraham, born to idolatrous parents, struggled and searched for many years until he finally discovered the One True G-d. He was persecuted and reviled by family and friends. Much of Mesopotamia turned against him. His was a lone voice, preaching to a hostile audience, until G-d compassionately directed him to Canaan, a land more conducive to his views.

Our Patriarch Jacob worked for his father-in-law, Laban, for twenty years, to marry and raise a family loyal to the Torah. During this time, he was manipulated, mocked, and deceived. Later, he was devastated by the loss of his son Joseph. Still later, he moved to Egypt during a famine, and died in a foreign land, so that his family, the fledgling future Jewish nation, might survive.

In Egypt, this family suffered for many generations, under harsh conditions of slavery, so that they might merit receiving the Torah. Their suffering refined and transformed them into a people worthy of G-d's Word. They gathered at Sinai and were finally given 613 commandments, each a glittering luminary, a star that radiates Divine light. Each commandment is a conduit through which G-d and the Jewish people connect and coalesce.

For many generations, our scholars and Sages taught Torah under the most trying conditions, often transmitting it at the cost of their livelihood, freedom, or even their lives. But they bequeathed us a vast corpus of Torah and a rich tapestry of commentary that guide our studies and observance to this very day.

VALIDATING THE SACRIFICE

Abraham forged the path of our destiny. Our ancestors paved that path with their suffering and sacrifice. The great scholars of Jewish history meticulously mapped our way, guiding us on the path to our destiny. When we reflect on the sacrifices that brought the Torah to our generation, we are suffused with gratitude to our ancestors, who sacrificed much, and to G-d, who permits us to benefit from their efforts.

Gratitude impels us to ensure, through the study of Torah, that their sacrifice was not in vain, and to actualize their dream by keeping the commandments. This opportunity is provided to us in luxury and freedom. We are not asked to sacrifice for it or to be worthy of it. We are asked simply to accept it. Accepting it demonstrates our gratitude; it validates their sacrifice.

If not for all those who came before, we would not be where we are today. To look back on our past is to take a lesson for the present and the future.

"What lessons we can learn from Jewish history?"

ETERNAL RAYS OF LIGHT

THE SUNSET

Sitting on the shores of Lake Huron, my family and I were enjoying a picturesque sunset. The sun, a spectacular ball of fire, painted the clear sky in hues of red, as it descended over the water. Enchanted by the majesty of the moment, my small daughter murmured, "Will there be a splash when it falls into the lake?" I explained that the sun wouldn't actually go into the lake; it would simply hide below the sky. Night would fall in Ontario, but beneath the horizon, the sun would continue to shine.

In my daughter's mind, though, the sun seemed to fall into the lake and the waters seemed to extinguish its light. Her words reminded me of King Solomon's wise dictum: "Mighty waters cannot extinguish love."[1]

ENDURING PASSION

Within every Jewish soul rages a fire of love for G-d, yet we are assailed by the riptides of mighty waters. These waters are the enticements of the evil inclination. On a national level, they are the surge of assimilation that has overwhelmed, even seemingly extinguished, the flame of many Jewish souls. Yet these waters, however mighty and turbulent, cannot extinguish the Jewish soul's innate passion for G-d.

Just as the sun is concealed by the lake's horizon, but not extinguished, so is our love for G-d only concealed, but not extinguished, by the floodwaters of assimilation. The fire of that love may be subdued, but beneath the surface,

---

[1] *Shir Hashirim* 8:7. This verse is chanted in the Haftarah of *Parshat Noach*. The Chassidic masters understood it as a reference to the mighty waters of Noah's Flood. Just as Noah survived the Flood, so will our passion for G-d ensure our survival despite today's Flood of assimilation.

the embers continue to glow. One day these embers will flare up again and, when they do, they will bathe our souls in the warm glow of fiery love.[2]

SUNRISES IN JEWISH HISTORY

After explaining that the sun's light had not been extinguished, I told my daughter that the next morning, we would see its light again. I was then reminded of another saying of King Solomon: "The sun rises and the sun sets, to its place it hastens and there it rises again."[3]

Jewish history is replete with sunrises and sunsets. Within this cycle, mercifully, there exists a rule: "Before the sun sets on one generation, it rises on another. On the day of Sarah's passing, Rebecca was born. Before the sun set on Moses, it rose on Joshua. On the day of Rabbi Akiva's passing, Rabbi Yehudah [the Nasi] was born."[4] Every time the sun sets on an illustrious Jewish leader, a new leader is born and the sun rises again.

This redeeming principle extends to other areas of Jewish life. After the passing of Rabbi Yehudah, the great centers of Torah study in the Land of Israel began to decline. But before these centers were completely closed down, the Torah centers of Babylon were established, attracting students from around the world. As the sun set on Torah study in the Land of Israel, it rose over Babylon.

Jewish history tells of four Babylonian Torah scholars who were taken captive on the high seas. They were ransomed to fledgling Jewish communities

---

[2] *Shir Hashirim Rabbah*, 8:7. There are several differences between the *Midrashic* text and the approach taken in this essay. The *Midrash* speaks of G-d's love for the Jewish people. Chassidic thought, however, quotes the *Zohar's* kabbalistic explanation that this verse relates to the love of Jews for G-d. See Torah Ohr p. 8b, where the floodwaters symbolize the constant grind of daily life, exacting their weary toll, rather than the tides of assimilation. For a resolution of the apparent conflict between these two interpretations, see Sefer Hamaamarim, 5717, p. 41.

[3] *Kohelet* 1:5.

[4] Kohelet Rabbah 1:5.

in Egypt, North Africa, Morocco, and Spain. What seemed at the time like a tragedy turned out to be Providential. All of these rabbis established major Torah academies in their new communities. When the illustrious *Rav Saadiah Gaon* passed away, the Babylonian academies, primary centers of Torah study for nearly six centuries, began to weaken. But even as their doors were closing, these new academies served as viable alternatives. As the sun set on Babylon, it rose elsewhere.[5]

HISTORY OF SUNSETS

On many occasions, it appeared to the nations of the world as if the sun was finally setting on our People.

Nebuchadnezzar of Babylon thought so, when his armies battered the walls of Jerusalem, torched the Temple, and exiled our people. Haman of Persia thought so, when he secured a royal edict to annihilate the Jewish nation. Antiochus Epiphanes of Syria thought so, when he outlawed Jewish practice and won over many Jews to Hellenism. Titus, and later Hadrian, of Rome thought so, when they conquered Judea and razed Jerusalem. Ferdinand of Spain thought so, when he expelled the Jews from Spain and prohibited observance of Jewish ritual. Bogdan Chmielnicki thought so, when his mobs led bloody pogroms across Eastern Europe. Hitler thought so when he attempted to "solve the Jewish Question." Iranian President, Mahmoud Ahmadinejad thinks so, as he calls for the destruction of Israel.

MY DAUGHTER'S FEARS

Even as night fell and darkness descended, I reassured my daughter that the sun would continue to shine. We, the Jewish people, are G-d's children; we too have no cause for fear. Even when our sun dips below the horizon, we can rest assured that soon, very soon, it will rise and shine again.

May we always merit seeing the morrow's rising sun. Jewish history teaches us that, regardless of how difficult our spiritual, emotional, fi-

---

[5] Sefer Hakabbalah.

nancial, or physical circumstances may become, we can trust in G-d and never despair.

"Raising children is one of life's greatest challenges. What does the Torah say, for example, about when we should discipline and when we should be lenient?"

SPARE THE ROD

THE DEBATE

Modern society has long debated the merit of corporal punishment. Generations of children were raised with it, but current popular psychology argues against it. Today, the rod is often spared even when children stubbornly refuse to comply with parental instruction.

What does Jewish law rule on this question? The Talmud teaches that parents and teachers may, on occasion, use corporal punishment to enforce discipline.[1] However an interesting Biblical episode seems to contradict this.

STRIKING THE ROCK

Accompanying our ancestors across the desert was a miraculous well that provided drinking water. On their arrival in the wilderness of Zin, the well dried out. Moses turned to G-d for direction. G-d instructed Moses to take his staff, gather the nation, and speak to the rock that it yield water. Moses gathered the nation and spoke briefly to the rock, but water did not come forth. Moses then raised his staff, struck the rock, and water gushed forth abundantly.[2] Moses provided water, but failed his test. G-d had instructed him to speak to the rock, but Moses used his staff instead. For striking the rock, Moses was severely punished.[3]

---

[1] *Babylonian Talmud, Makot* 8a; *Yad Hachazakah, Hilchot Rotzeach* 5 and *Hilchot Talmud Torah* 4.

[2] *Numbers* 20:11. See Rashi's commentary ibid.

[3] Had he talked to the rock, the people would have taken note that even a rock, that neither hears nor sees, obeys the Divine command. They would have reasoned: How much more so should a human being obey G-d. Rashi on *Numbers* 20:12.

This story seems to support the contemporary opposition to corporal punishment, contradicting the above-stated Talmudic dictum. Moses was punished for using the rod, because force should never be an option where words might suffice.[4]

WHEN THE HEART IS CLOSED

I would argue that the key lies in the object that Moses struck. Moses struck a rock, and that was wrong. Because a rock-like student must never be struck. What is a rock-like student?

In the Torah, the word "rock" usually refers to the heart. The Torah says, "And I shall remove the heart of stone from within you."[5] A heart of stone is a closed heart. Rabbi Akiva, the greatest Sage of our history, had a heart that was at first closed to Torah. In his youth, Rabbi Akiva refused to study Torah. One day, however, he observed a trickle of water that had, after many years, formed a depression in the rock face on which it had dripped. Rabbi Akiva reflected that if water-drops could erode a surface of rock, surely words of Torah could make an impact even on a heart of stone. Rabbi Akiva then entered the academy and became our greatest scholar.[6]

If Rabbi Akiva had been physically forced to attend the rabbinical academy, would the words of Torah have penetrated his heart? Surely not! A closed heart is immune to force. In the event of force it clams up completely, and stubbornly refuses to open. A closed heart can be influenced only through gentle, loving words, spoken from the heart, not through the rod. Our Sages

---

[4] One might wonder why it was necessary to carry the staff if he was not intended to use it. The commentators offer many answers. I would add the following story: In the memoirs of the former Lubavitcher Rebbe, a story is told of a teacher who was loved by his students. This teacher never used the rod, but he did hang a lash on the wall. Every time the students misbehaved, he would glance at the lash, and the students would immediately take the hint.

[5] *Yechezkel* 36:26.

[6] *Avot D'Rebbi Natan* 6.

taught that words spoken from the heart always enter the heart they are spoken to.

This is true of a student whose heart is closed, but whose mind is open. What of the student whose mind is closed but whose heart is open? Words can enter a closed heart, but can words enter a closed mind?

WHEN THE MIND IS CLOSED

Words alone cannot restrain a mother from rushing into a blazing inferno to find her missing child. Nothing short of physical restraint can impede her headlong rush. This is because, at that moment, she is controlled by her heart; her mind is closed to reason. Words of reason cannot enter a mind that is closed to reason.

A child, who has yet to mature intellectually, is controlled by emotion more than intellect. Words are simply inadequate for a child in the flow of emotional outburst. On occasion, when the mind is closed and emotion pours forth, the child requires restraint, not reason. When a child, driven purely by emotion, repeatedly fails to obey instruction and wanders out into dangerous roads s/he is, at least momentarily, impervious to verbal instruction. When the mind is closed and the heart is wide open, the only effective language is a touch of physical discipline.

THE ART OF ADMINISTRATION

The Talmud teaches that a teacher may project a stern air, to inspire awe in his students and spur them to greater achievement. Far from giving the teacher free rein with the rod, we note that these words were carefully chosen. License is not given to be a stern teacher, merely to project a stern air.

As parents and teachers, we must always hold our own negative emotions in careful check. Even as we appear angry to our students we must never feel that way within. We must never administer physical discipline in anger. On the contrary, a teacher's heart must be filled with bitterness over having been forced to resort to physical discipline.

A TELLING TALE

Chassidic lore tells of a young boy who threw pebbles at roosters and was disciplined by his father for hurting the birds. After delivering several lashes, the father retired to his quarters where he broke down and wept. The child's violent behavior had warranted corrective discipline, but it wasn't the lashes that had the most impact on the little boy. From his own room, the child heard his father's wrenching sobs.

This broke the child's heart and cleansed his soul. He entered his father's room and approached him with contrition. He kissed the hand that had struck him, and embraced his father tightly. The child never needed to be disciplined again. He was changed forever.

It wasn't the rod that inspired the child to become a gentle and kind soul. It was the love with which it was administered.[7]

---

[7] Lubavitcher Rebbe's Memoirs, vol. I, p. 266.

Bibliography

Abarbanel
Rabbi Don Isaac Abarbanel
Spain, 1437-1508
Torah Commentary

Avodat Yisrael
Rabbi Yisrael Haupstein
Koznitz, 1737-1814
Chassidic Commentary on Torah

Avot D'R. Nosson
Talmudic Sages
Ethical Teachings

Rabbenu Bachye
Rabbi Bachye ben Asher
Saragossa, Spain, 1255-1340
Torah Commentary

Sefer Baal Shem Tov Al Hatorah
Rabbi Yisrael Ben Eliezer, Founder of the
Chassidic Movement
Medzeboz, Ukraine, 1698 – 1760
Chassidic Commentary on Torah

B'er Mayim Chayim
Rabbi Chaim Tirar, Chernowitz
1760 - 1817)
Chassidic Commentary on Torah

Bet Halevi
Rabbi Yoseph Ber Soloveitchik
Slutzk, 1820- 1892
Torah Commentary

Bet Rebbe
Rabbi Chaim Meyer Hillman
Kehot Publication Society, NY, 1953.
History of Chabad

Chafetz Chayim
Rabbi Israel Meir Kagan
Radin, 1838 -1933
Against Gossip and Slander

Chidushei Aggadot
R. Yehudah Loew
Prague, 1525 -1609
Talmudic Commentary

The Committed Life
Rebbetzin Esther Jungreis
Harper Collins Pub., S. Francisco, 1998
Jewish Morals and Ethics

Crown of Creation
Mrs. Channah Weisburg, Mosaic Press,
Buffalo, NY, 1996.
Jewish Women

Derech Hashem
R. Moshe Chaim Luzzatto
Padua, Italy, 1707 – 1746
Mystical Teachings

Divrei Yisrael Al Hatorah
Rabbi Yisrael of Maditz, 1901
Chassidic Commentary on Torah

Ethics of our Fathers
Mishnah, Tractate, Avot
Ethical Torah Teachings

Sefer Gevurot Hashem
R. Yehudah Loew
Prague, 1525-1609
Jewish Ethics and Philosophy

Sefer Hachinuch,
The anonymous author, who identifies
himself only as "a Levite from Barcelo-
na," was a student of Rabbi Shlomo ben
Aderet, in the thirteenth century
The 613 Commandments

Sefer Hakabbalah
Rabbi Abraham Ibn Daud
Toledo, 1110 - 1180
Mystical Teachings

Hayom Yom
Kehot Publication Society, 1943
Chassidic Thoughts for Every Day

Sefer Hitvaaduot - Torat Menachem
Rabbi Menachem M Schneerson, Rebbe
of Lubavitch, 1902 - 1994
Talks of the Lubavitcher Rebbe

Horeb
Soncino Press, New
York/London/Jerusalem
Rabbi Samson Raphael Hirsch
Frankfurt, 1808 - 1888
Jewish Ethics and Philosophy

Ibn Izra
Rabbi Abraham ben Meir ibn Ezra
Spain, 1092 –1167
Torah Commentary

Ikarim
Rabbi Yosef Albo
Spain, 1380 - 1444
Jewish Ethics and Philosophy

Kedushat Levi
Rabbi Levi Yitzhak
Berdichev, 1740 - 1810
Chassidic Commentary on Torah

Ktav Sofer
Rabbi Avraham Shmuel Binyamin Sofer
Pressburg, 1815 -1879
Torah Commentary

Kli Yakar
Rabbi Ephraim Shlomo of Luntshitz,
1550 - 1619
Torah Commentary

Likutei Diburim
Rabbi YY Schneerson, Sixth Rebbe of
Lubavitch, 1880 - 1950
Talks of the Previous Lubavitcher Rebbe

Likutei Sichot
Rabbi Menachem M Schneerson, Rebbe
of Lubavitch, 1902 - 1994
Torah and Chassidic Commentary

Sefer HaMitzvot
Maimonides, Rabbi Moshe ben Maimon
Egypt, 1135 - 1204
The 613 Commandments

Sefer Hatoda'ah
Eliyahu Ki-Tov
Israel, 1912 – 1976
Jewish Holidays

Sefer Maamarim 5704
Rabbi YY Schneerson Sixth Rebbe of
Lubavitch, 1880 - 1950
Chassidic Discourses

Sefer Mamarim Admur Hazaken
Rabbi Schneur Zalman, founder of Cha-
bad Chassidsm
Liadi, 1745 - 1812
Chassidic Discourses

Sefer Hamamaarim Melukat
Rebbe Menachem M Schneerson, Rebbe
of Lubavitch, 1902 - 1994
Chassidic Discourses

Machshevet Hachassidut
Rabbi Yoel Kahn
 Sifriyat Eshel, 1961.
Chassidic Thought on Torah

Magen Avraham
Rebbe Avraham Abeli Gumbiner
Kalish, 1637 - 1683
Halacha

Magid Devarav Leyaakov
Rabbi Dov Ber
Mezritch, 1700-1772
Chassidic Thought on Torah

Maharsha
Rabbi Shmuel Eliezer Edels
Posen, 1555 – 1631
Talmudic Commentary

Maor Einayim
Rabbi Nachum of Chernobyl, 1730 - 1797
Chassidic Commentary on Torah

Malbim
Rabbi Meir Leib ben Yechiel Michael
Russia 1809 - 1879
Torah Commentary

Memoirs of the Previous Lubavitcher
Rebbe
Rabbi YY Shcneerson, Sixth Rebbe of
Lubavitch, 1880 - 1950
History of Early Chassidim

Midrash Tanchumah
Talmudic Sages
Midrashic Teachings on Torah

Midrash Rabbah
Talmudic Sages
Midrashic Teachings on Torah

Mishnah Brurah
Rabbi Israel Meir Kagan
Radin, 1838 - 1933
Halacha

Moreh Nevuchim
Maimonides, Rabbi Moshe ben Maimon
Egypt, 1135 - 1204
Jewish Philosophy

Mystical Concepts in Chassidus
Dr. Immanuel Jacob Schochet
Kehot Publication Soceity, 1988
Chassidic Thought

Noam Elimelech
Rabbi Elimelech of Lujzinsk 1717 – 1787
Chassidic Commentary on Torah

Or Hachayim
Rabbi Chaim Ibn Atar
Morocco, 1696 - 1743
Torah Commentary

Ohr Hatorah
Rabbi Menachem M Schneerson, Third
Rebbe of Lubavitch, 1789 - 1866
Chassidic Commentary on Torah

Panim Yafot
Rabbi Pinchas Horowitz
Frankfurt, 1730 - 1805
Torah Commentary

P'nei Yehoshua
Rabbi Yaakov Yusha Falik
Frankfurt, 1781 – 1956
Talmudic Commentary

Peninim M'shulchan Ha'gra
Rabbi Eliyahu Gaon
Vilna, 1720 – 1782
Torah Commentary

Ramban
Nachmanides, Rabbi Moshe Ben
Nachman
Spain 1194 - 1270
Torah Commentary

Rashi
Rabbi Shlomo Yitzchaki
France, 1040 - 1105
Torah and Talmudic Commentary

Rectifying the State of Israel
Rabbi Yitzchack Ginsburgh
Gal Einai Institute, Israel, 2002
Mystical Thoughts on the Land of Israel

Sifri
Talmudic Sages
Talmudic Teachings on Torah

Rosh Emunah
Rabbi Don Isaac Abarbanel
Spain, 1437 - 1508
Jewish Philosophy

S'fat Emet
Rabbi Yehudah Aryeh Leib Alter
Gur, 1847 – 1905
Torah Commentary

Shemirat Halashon
Rabbi Israel Meir Kagan
Radin, 1838 - 1933
Against Gossip and Slander

Shem Mishmuel
Rabbi Shmuel Borenstein
Sochaczev, 1855 - 1927
Chassidic Commentary on Torah

Taam Vadaat
Rabbi Moshe Shternbech, Jerusalem
Torah Commentary

Tanya
Rabbi Schneur Zalman, founder of Cha-
bad Chassidsm, Liadi, 1745 - 1812
Chassidic Thought

Tiferet Yonatan
Rabbi Yonatan Eibescutz
Prague, 1690 - 1764
Torah Commentary

Torah Or
Rabbi Schneur Zalman, founder of Cha-
bad Chassidsm, Liadi, 1745 - 1812
Chassidic Commentary on Torah

Torat Chayim
Rabbi Duber, Second Rebbe of Lubav-
itch, 1788 – 1828
Chassidic Commentary on Torah

Torat Kohanim
Talmudic Sages
Talmudic Teachings on Torah

Torat Menachem
Rabbi Menachem M Schneerson, Rebbe
of Lubavitch, 1902 - 1994
Talks of the Lubavitcher Rebbe

Torat Moshe
Rabbi Moshe Sofer
Pressburg, 1762 - 1838
Torah Commentary

Torat Moshe
Rabbi Moshe Alshich
Tzefat, 1508 - 1600
Torah Commentary

Torah Temimah
Rabbi Baruch HaLevi Epstein
Pinsk, 1860 - 1941
Torah Commentary

Yad Hachazakah,
Maimonides, Rabbi Moshe ben Maimon
Egypt, 1135 - 1204
Halacha

Yalkut Shimoni
Talmudic Sages
Midrashic Teachings on Torah